The Insider's Guide to

Credit

Repair

The Insider's Guide to
Credit
Repair

By K.E. Varner

CAREER
PRESS

Franklin Lakes, NJ

THE INSIDER'S GUIDE TO CREDIT REPAIR
EDITED AND TYPESET BY CHRISTOPHER CAROLEI
Cover design by Johnson Design
Printed in the U.S.A. by Book-mart Press

To order this title, please call toll-free 1-800-CAREER-1 (NJ and Canada: 201-848-0310) to order using VISA or MasterCard, or for further information on books from Career Press.

The Career Press, Inc., 3 Tice Road, PO Box 687,
Franklin Lakes, NJ 07417
www.careerpress.com

Library of Congress Cataloging-in-Publication Data

Varner, K.E., 1976-
   The insider's guide to credit repair / by K.E. Varner.
      p. cm.
   Includes bibliographical references and index.
   ISBN 1-56414-809-2 (paper)
      1. Consumer credit—Handbooks, manuals, etc. 2. Finance, Personal—Handbooks, manuals, etc. I. Title.

HG3755.V37 2005
332.7'43--dc22

2005042073

Dedication

I dedicate this to consumers and everyone involved in consumer awareness and education. This is also dedicated to Dorothy Mae Varner: though we sometimes fall short, your legacy of hard work, family love and self-respect will never perish; we love you.

Acknowledgments

Thanks to the most High for the opportunity, strength, determination and belief in myself. Bridget Dent—your loyalty and wisdom are insurmountable! Thank you for your vision, motivation and prayers. I greatly appreciate your advice and friendship. LeRhonda C. Manigault—your understanding of my intentions for this project cannot be surpassed. I value the sincerity you've shown by challenging my thinking. Thank you for helping me learn how to make intuitive decisions in my career that in some capacity resulted in the creation of this book. Thanks for your friendship and love. Anthony Brown—thank you for urging me to seriously consider writing. You're the epitome of an educator. Kira Reed—your thoughtfulness and faith is undeniable, and you've shown me over and over again what true friendship is. Sheraldon Graves, Lillian Russell, Emily Tucker, Margaree Limehouse, Deborah Eley, Edith Torres, Elaina Padilla, Carmen Sawn, Atresa Carr—thanks for the encouragement and inspiration. Precious Jones, Anthony Smith, Carlos Quinones, Deon DeSouza, Charlotte Reeves-Oyebanji, Vanessa Linning-Shuler—thanks for your relentless support. Finally, many thanks to my publisher, Career Press, for believing in this project, and thanks to Michael Lewis for his candid feedback and Christopher Carolei for his courtesy in making my wants and needs a priority.

Contents

Foreword   11

Chapter 1: An Overview of Credit   19

Chapter 2: Establishing Credit and Responsibility   35

Chapter 3: Credit Reports   53

Chapter 4: Establishing Utility Services Using Credit   73

Chapter 5: Credit-Reporting Agencies   83

Chapter 6: Credit Scoring   99

Chapter 7: Bargaining With Your Creditors   121

Chapter 8: Correcting Errors on Credit Reports   133

Chapter 9: Restoring Credit Through
            Consumer Counseling   147

Chapter 10: Avoiding Identity Theft and Fraud:
            Reclaiming Your Status   159

Chapter 11: Seeking Help From Credit Doctors   179

Chapter 12: Credit Laws for All Purposes:
           Knowing Your Rights   191

Chapter 13: Complaints and Litigation
           Create Changes   215

Chapter 14: Helpful Information   223

Afterword   241

Appendix   253

Glossary   267

References   275

Index   279

About the Author   285

Foreword

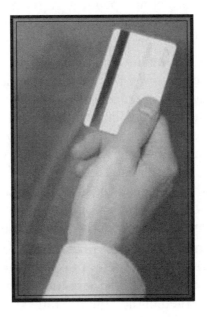

It is imperative that consumers understand how repayment habits affect their creditworthiness and how the network of furnishers, credit reporting, credit counseling and government organizations function and cooperate to maintain a successful process.

U.S. consumers are chronic spenders and users of credit who incur high levels of debt. In fact, consumer debt is at a record-level high, doubling over the past 10 years. To help spur a weakening economy, the Federal Reserve of our government often lowers interest rates.

Lowering interest rates encourages consumers to purchase on credit. On one hand, this helps stimulate the economy; on the other, it opens a door for many consumers to easily acquire more debt. Recent studies show that nearly 40 percent of consumers trading in cars owe more on the vehicle than it is actually worth.

In addition to consumers acquiring record levels of debt, they are not saving as much as they are spending. At the present time, Americans spend more than 18 percent of after-tax income paying debts, while only 2 percent of that income is reserved for personal savings.

Oddly enough, consumers tend to use lower interest rates as opportunities to purchase more (such as finer homes or cars) than as opportunities to save and/or reduce expenses. For example, if automobile dealerships offer 0 percent financing, most consumers deduce that the best way to take advantage of the low rate is by purchasing a more elegant car (the one they've always wanted but could not afford). In this case, instead of returning to the neighborhood in a Chevy, Jane Consumer cruises back to Smallville in a Caddy. Because the low rate was applied to a more luxurious car, Jane has not realized any savings (provided her income and other financial obligations remain unchanged).

One key adverse consequence of elevated consumer debt is the steady augmentation of bankruptcy filings that are not business related. Personal bankruptcies compose the overwhelming majority of all bankruptcies filed in the United States. In the past 10 years, bankruptcy rates have doubled, while personal savings have declined by 50 percent.

The U.S. economy thrives on consumer spending—spending that accounts for nearly three-quarters of the U.S. gross domestic product and roughly one-fifth of the world gross domestic product. As spending and dependency on credit continues to increase, so does the need for consumers to understand personal credit management.

In creating this material I was not motivated by disdain or disapproval of the credit process or system. Rather, I thought there was the need for a credible piece of material that could bring some understanding and value to consumers regarding the management of personal credit. The intention to reveal the practical truth rather than fallacies about establishing, maintaining and rebuilding credit is one of the most influential forces behind the formulation of this piece. My experiences in working for a major credit-reporting agency and service provider, alike, revealed to me how misinformed many consumers are about personal credit. While interacting with consumers on various levels, I was astounded by the incorrect information they regarded as gospel. This realization urged me to take a closer look at what credible resources were available to consumers wishing to learn about credit management. My investigation yielded disappointing results. I concluded that very little helpful information and very few forums exist that aid consumers in understanding their credit—and even less about managing and restoring it.

Credit-reporting agencies are often so occupied with compliance of state and federal laws that they're unable to provide the type of educational assistance needed by most consumers. It should be clarified that credit-reporting agencies do not exist in whole to serve and educate consumers; this is merely a portion of their enormous responsibility. They also have customers to serve, those being furnishers of information and credit grantors that subscribe to their services. Unfortunately, the laws regulating credit-reporting agencies allow little time for them to deviate and become more engaged in the consumer education process.

Some consumers have even expressed feeling rushed when contacting credit-reporting agencies. To some degree this may be true, as the agencies are consumed with average hold times, speed of answer times and block rates that the government regulates and holds them accountable for reaching. In most cases, the personnel are coached regularly to be succinct in their communication and get consumers on their way as quickly as possible. This may be a byproduct of regulation as well as the ever-unattainable goal of keeping consumer service centers properly staffed.

As there are opportunities for credit-reporting agencies, there are also opportunities for furnishers, credit grantors and credit-counseling organizations to aid with consumer education. Unfortunately, these entities have their own agendas and motivations, most of which do not dedicate ample time to expanding consumers' knowledge of credit, building it and reestablishing it. Although a number of them may provide some credit-education services, far too many furnishers and creditors view the credit-reporting system as a method of recouping payment and a tool of punishment for failing to repay, second only to validating a consumer's eligibility to receive credit. And as of late, some credit-counseling services have received bad publicity for failing to adequately assist consumers with debt management and credit awareness. Some argue that it is the essence of frustration and confusion that keeps the credit-reporting system thriving so vibrantly. On the other hand, it is this type of chaos that helps solidify consumers' ignorance and misuse of credit.

The missing link is consumer education. Make no mistake about it: the consumer market alone is the most lucrative of them all. Most businesses and our economy would crumble without the revenue generated by consumer spending and/or the profit potential offered through the exchange of consumer information. Knowing how to properly manage personal credit will add value to your life and make your journey to financial freedom a whole lot easier.

How this book will help you

By understanding credit and how to manage it, and by knowing the key players that keep it functioning, consumers will be empowered to challenge flaws and/or loopholes in the system that typically contribute to perpetual confusion or sometimes downright injustice. These consumers will have the ability to rectify their own credit woes and get back on the road to managing it wisely. An educated consumer will know the potential consequences that may follow as a result of their success or negligence. The enlightened consumer will act and speak with complete confidence in dealings with creditors, collectors and consumer-reporting agencies alike. This consumer will be equipped to handle most, if not all, affairs related to personal credit, sparing the expense and time of dealing with a credit doctor.

This book was written to provide accurate information about consumer credit management, credit reporting and all of the major players involved in the consumer information industry. As well as being a tool of enlightening information, this book will focus on the preventative aspects of managing credit and offer solutions to many of the problems consumers face with restoring it. The path to great credit begins with education!

Every effort has been made to provide truth and accuracy as they relate to this subject, though it is possible that some things may change even by the time this material is published. The information contained in this book has been carefully researched and communicated to ensure the highest level of credibility and understanding to its readers.

This book was not written to instruct consumers on how to manipulate the credit-reporting system in an attempt to get true, negative entries expunged from their credit records. It was written to educate consumers on how to *prevent* credit blemishes and correct *errors* appearing on their credit records that hold them from obtaining the goods, services or luxuries they deserve.

In addition to providing expert advice on repairing one's credit, it will tackle other vital areas of consumer credit needed to maintain positive financial status, such as establishing credit, protecting and recovering from the pitfalls of identity theft and credit fraud, as well as credit scoring, just to name a few. This book will tell you how to permanently correct mistakes on your credit record the right way. It will take the subject a step further by focusing on understanding the credit process and teaching you how to head off credit problems before they even arise by bargaining with your creditors. Doing so is always less exacerbating and more inexpensive than trying to correct or change a pattern of behavior marked by swindling creditors and credit-reporting agencies.

The negative perception of the term "credit repair"

In the credit industry there is a negative connotation associated with the term "credit repair." The dark perception surrounding credit repair has been caused in large by a number of unscrupulous businesses that have stolen money from consumers and made the jobs of creditors, furnishers and reporting agencies more burdensome. They are guilty of promising to wipe away true, negative credit entries appearing on consumers' credit reports. Typically they charge consumers money for their services but rarely deliver the desired, expected results. This has left many consumers alienated and broke, with few alternatives other than making complaints to local, state and federal authorities.

For the record, there is no legal way to have correct information removed from a credit record except through a credit-reporting agency, a court of law or a provider of information. Further, most of these businesses that thrive do so at the mercy of consumer ignorance and desperation. At best, they offer temporary fixes to long-term problems that continue to persist as a result of miseducation and unhealthy, poor handling of debt obligations.

In addition, teaching consumers exclusively how to beat the system encourages irresponsible, unscrupulous behavior and ensures that many of these organizations will continue to remain in business. You cannot correct or amend what is already accurate, whether it's positive or negative. The paradigm of credit repair, as it is known, must shift from the negative reputation of manipulation that has been furthered by some organizations known as "credit doctors," to one of consumer empowerment and self-help that will be promoted by this book.

While preparing this material, I read a number of books that concentrated primarily on teaching tactics to suppress negative credit entries that are true and on lambasting furnishers of credit and credit-reporting agencies. As I read them, I highlighted, underlined and made many notes negating the claims they made. Once again, I was amazed by the amount of inaccurate information being provided to consumers. The factors that set me and my material apart from other publications are my position, intent and credentials.

Help is here

The bottom line is there are many organizations out there that do not have consumers' best interests in mind. The obvious question is: "Where can consumers turn for help?" Look no further, because help is here!

While I acknowledge that many opportunities for consumer misuse and abuse exist in the consumer credit industry, I do not oppose the process or the system entirely. I believe that, if used correctly, all parties could benefit from the credit industry substantially. If educating consumers about managing credit equates to negatively impacting the profitability of organizations that take advantage of consumers, I gladly accept the challenge. This is one of few personal finance books designed to teach and help and will set itself apart from many of the potboilers that have done nothing more than mislead and frustrate consumers. If bringing into fruition the raw truth equates to educating and uplifting consumers by going against the grain, I also welcome this opportunity. Regardless of the label associated, I express these ideas and advice through my firsthand experience, with candor, dignity and integrity. It is my only goal to help mold a knowledgeable, confident and responsible consumer class, who can remain undaunted by misinformation and the perceived authority of corporate entities.

Relying on my experience in the credit industry and the different capacities in which I have functioned, I believe the knowledge I share will be of infinite value to consumers. My days of interacting with consumers equipped me with the ability to identify their wants, needs and frustrations with credit and the rebuilding process. Consumers desire fair treatment, simplicity and honesty from all parties involved in the credit industry. They want to know how to mend mistakes. Many feel as though the process of correcting errors is convoluted and designed to keep them perplexed. They have a need to understand the benefits of credit, the roles of the credit players, and the long-term results of not managing credit responsibly. They also need to know how to avoid credit problems.

Among other responsibilities, I have appeared in federal court to represent a credit-reporting agency with legal counsel in mediation efforts. I learned that it is very unfortunate that the agencies still carry the heaviest burden of responsibility in cases involving erroneous information in consumer credit reports.

My consumer credit experience and desire to educate have served as a foundation for composing this material. Through these efforts and others, I hope to continue contributing to the eradication of a befuddled, thirsty consumer class. Even more, this shall serve to educate, broaden and stimulate the minds of those seeking more than a mediocre overview of the complex maze of personal credit management.

My promise to readers is to equip them with the knowledge needed to liberate them (in some capacity) from credit dependency and the vulnerabilities associated with lack of understanding. I ask that my readers approach the material as if it were a brand-new theory or concept not yet endorsed by proponents but also not yet protested by opponents. Approach this information in the same manner that you learned the alphabet. I implore you to release all of the rumors, fallacies and doubts about personal credit that have been embedded into your mind to create and maintain fear, mystery and chaos. Share this material and your understanding of it with your children, students, coworkers and acquaintances alike. Read it, think about it, and absorb it. But, most of all, reinforce your understanding by exercising the strength and power of the knowledge you've acquired. Welcome to *The Insider's Guide to Credit Repair*!

An Overview
of Credit

Defining and understanding credit

This chapter will explain what credit is, discuss the benefits of credit to consumers and our economy at large and identify the important parties involved in consumer credit.

The Major Players

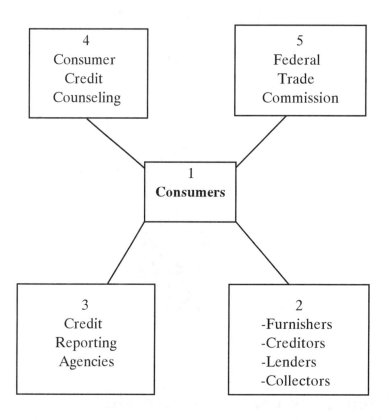

"Credit" is best defined as an item of value that is given to another for care, protection or performance. The concept behind credit is: "Receive now and pay later." When an applicant is approved for a credit card, the issuing company is entrusting the card, with its available purchasing power, to a consumer. As opposed to issuing the card for care and protection, the merchant's primary motive for extending credit is performance and, of course, to make a profit. In this context, performing would consist of a consumer using the credit card to make purchases. This is what the card issuer wants consumers to do. The idea of "receiving now and paying later" allows most people to enjoy luxuries of a higher standard of living. How many of us would be able to visit the local Lexus dealer and pay for a new car with spot cash? Not many, I gather. Credit allows us to protract our repayment obligation over a period of time (sometimes defined and other times not), thereby alleviating the burden of responsibility of an immediate debt. Credit allows us the comfort and convenience of shopping online, via telephone, through catalogs and so on. In fact, in some areas individuals cannot even receive movie rental memberships without guaranteeing them with a credit card. Rental cars and vehicles used to aid in moving must also be reserved with credit or debit cards. In this light, credit offers consumers a variety of products and services that would otherwise be inaccessible or at least difficult to enjoy.

Banks and various loan institutions also benefit through the use of credit. While they may not require full payment of a debt up front, they earn money from finance charges, over-the-limit fees, late fees (which have gradually increased over time) and other charges that they impose. Upon accepting a loan, a consumer is agreeing to repay a bank for not only the original amount of the loan, but also any finance charges that may have been assessed based upon his or her credit history and other factors. Financing of most loans is fixed, meaning that it cannot change unless the debt is refinanced. Credit cards, however, work a bit differently. The annual percentage rates may change based upon various factors, such as the end of a promotion, occurrence of a late payment made by a cardholder, adverse or positive review of a cardholder's credit history by issuing company and so forth. Some of these factors could actually result in a consumer receiving a more competitive annual percentage rate than he or she previously had. For example, sometimes we receive letters from our existing banks or credit card providers informing us that they have increased our credit limits due to good payment history. Be wary: a higher credit limit sounds tantalizing, but its primary purpose is to heighten your debt. Higher credit limits equal higher risks for most consumers. What they do not mention is that they have also reviewed our credit records. This is perfectly legal. When we enter into contracts with issuers of credit (meaning, we accept the card), we are giving them authorization to review our credit histories as often as they would like during the life of the account. However, don't be alarmed! These types of credit reviews (frequently referred to as "soft inquiries") are not detrimental to your overall credit rating. Credit reviews (more commonly called "inquiries") will be discussed in greater detail in an upcoming chapter. On the other hand, if a bank assesses an adverse review of your credit, you may receive a letter advising that your annual percentage rate has increased, your credit limit has been decreased, or even worse, your account has been closed. Consumers must always read the fine print on all credit applications for loans and cards.

Most consumers regard credit as an intricate and confusing concept. This approach is taken because people generally fear the unknown. Enlightened, educated and savvy consumers understand how credit works and the importance of it. By understanding credit and viewing it in a mutualistic manner, it is actually not such a bad concept after all. Credit offers both merchants and consumers a variety of benefits.

The credit-reporting system and the major players

I. Credit-reporting agencies

Credit-reporting agencies are charged with collecting, storing and maintaining information on consumers and some businesses. The agencies primarily store debt repayment patterns of consumers, but some may also store and report debt repayment behavior of small businesses. Traditionally, credit-reporting companies have been known to focus on consumers' payment patterns. However, in more recent times, it is becoming increasingly common for them to break into the business credit-reporting market, particularly the small business sector.

Dun & Bradstreet is a credit-reporting agency that currently only reports debt repayment patterns of businesses, versus consumers. Until recently, Dun & Bradstreet has never been confronted with competition from any of the three major, national credit-reporting agencies. It will be interesting to see if any of the traditional consumer-reporting agencies will become a top contender of Dun & Bradstreet in business credit reporting. Because these agencies (Trans Union, Experian, and Equifax) may report information about consumers and businesses alike, I find it appropriate to refer to all of them as "credit-reporting agencies" as opposed to "consumer-reporting agencies" (the traditional term). Many governmental bodies, written laws, furnishers, as well as consumers may refer to them as consumer-reporting agencies (in the spirit of tradition), but I find it necessary to distinguish between their different connotations for the sake of clarity.

II. Furnishers

Furnishers of credit are the sources of information that credit-reporting agencies use in constructing credit reports. Including a host of different businesses and organizations, they run the gamut. Some of them are local, state and federal courts; creditors, which include credit unions, banks, finance companies, credit card companies, utility service providers, wireless communication providers, check verification companies, mortgage companies, student loan lenders, various retailers and department stores; and collection agencies. Some of these suppliers do not proactively submit information to the credit-reporting companies (courts) but often assist them in verifying the accuracy of public record filings appearing on consumers' credit reports during reinvestigations. The furnishers' information may appear in various sections of a credit report. The legal system does not normally utilize the credit-reporting agencies' databases to assist them with conducting their business. There is only one exception that comes to mind. For example, a court may gain access to a credit-reporting agency's database in order to locate a consumer. The need of a court to locate a consumer may be to send a subpoena, an order or notice of child support or other legal matters that require contacting a consumer in writing.

III. The government

Of course, no major public or private industry is spared the government's scrutiny. I'm definitely not suggesting that governmental intervention is a bad idea; in some cases, without its assistance and insight, weaker sides would certainly be at a disadvantage. The Federal Trade Commission is a division of the U.S. government that enforces laws related to the credit industry, particularly the Fair Credit Reporting Act. This body of the government can be thought of as the umpire, making rulings in the game between the following two teams:

Team 1	vs.	Team 2
-Credit-reporting		Consumers
agencies		
-Furnishers		
-Service Providers		

Consumers' rights and power have been leveraged quite effectively, largely due to action taken on their behalf by the Federal Trade Commission—especially in cases that they demonstrated non-compliance of any portion of the Fair Credit Reporting Act. This entity will be considered in more detail in an upcoming chapter. For the moment, the goal is to become acquainted with the most active and powerful players engaged in the consumer credit industry.

IV. Consumer credit counselors

Consumer credit counseling agencies assist consumers with financial education and debt-management solutions. Most, if not all, are nonprofit organizations that depend heavily on a network of credit grantors for financial support. While they do not stand independently and some may question their influence, if channeled appropriately and with integrity, these bodies could supply a wealth of assistance to consumers through their services. Therefore, they are listed as the fourth players in the credit-reporting process.

V. Consumers

Consumers provide the core existence of the credit-reporting system. They are the purchasers and users of credit. Their information (habits, interests, and so on) and spending activity allow all the other players to reap profits. In turn, services provided by the other players allow consumers to immediately enjoy benefits that they would otherwise have to forego temporarily, if not indefinitely. As noted previously, consumer spending is a requirement to maintaining a strong economy, nationally and beyond. If consumer spending halts, the impact can be severe. There are millions of consumer credit reports existing in the databases of reporting agencies. Obviously there are many more players on team 2 (the consumer group) than there are on team 1 (the non-consumer group).

The concept of "what's in it for me, what's in it for you" is the key motivating factor that keeps the two teams united on some level, even though they may dissent on others. Failure to execute or act fairly in carrying out an agreement is the root cause of most, if not all dissatisfaction involving the teams. Each one of the players has challenges. Let's take a look at the primary opportunities each of them faces, some being shared responsibilities and others being individual.

Credit-reporting agencies carry the burden of making sure the information they report is complete and accurate. They are also responsible for protecting the information they maintain and access to it. Furnishers are charged with making sure the information they supply to credit-reporting agencies is complete and accurate. They too are responsible for protecting the information they supply and access to it.

The challenges that the Federal Trade Commission faces are ensuring fairness in all credit practices, as broad as they may be, and providing educational assistance to consumers. Consumer credit counselors are charged with assessing consumers' financial situations and determining the best course of action to follow. Their challenges are to regain credibility among consumers and restore integrity to their services that have become tainted with ulterior motives and poor practices of some agency members. Lastly, consumers are responsible for making sure they fulfill their ends of agreements. Quite frankly, they are responsible for repaying their debts on time and as agreed with creditors. In addition, they are charged with safeguarding their personal information as best as possible.

Three basic types of credit

There are three fundamental types of credit accounts: open, installment and revolving. Let's spend some time discussing each of them.

Open accounts are accounts that require full payment for services received at the end of each billing cycle. These types of accounts will never request a minimum payment. Examples of open accounts include:

- Gas cards (such as Shell, Amoco).

- Utility accounts (telephone, gas, electricity).

- Cellular accounts (Verizon and Nextel, for example).

Installment accounts are ones that have a fixed monthly repayment amount. The amount of the payment can only change if the debt has been refinanced. Examples of installment accounts are:

- Student loans.

- Auto loans.

- Personal loans.

- Mortgage loans.

- Recreational merchandise loans (boats, motorcycles, and so on).

Directions to Credit Street

Creditors Blvd.

Consumer Street

Federal Trade
Commision Ave.

Credit Reporting Rd.

Consumer Street

Credit
Counseling Place

Revolving accounts require a minimum payment of a larger existing balance at the end of the monthly billing cycle. They do not require full payment of a balance owed at the end of each billing period, however, any unpaid amount that carries over is subject to addition charges. Revolving accounts include, for instance:

- Credit cards (such as Visa and Master Card).

- Department store/retail cards (such as Sears, JC Penney, Macy's, Best Buy and Circuit City).

Revolving accounts are often accused of being the inducers of bad credit. The truth is that credit cards must be used wisely and, when they are, can have very effective bargaining power. Basic advice is to never charge an amount on a credit card that exceeds your ability to repay it in full within 30 days. This is the golden rule! If the amount is repaid in full at the end of the billing cycle, no additional charges will be assessed. This is often where creditors "trick us," so to speak. They offer a minimum amount due, but subsequently attach charges to the remaining unpaid balance that carries over to the next billing period. This technique, along with late fees, annual membership fees, and so on, is what allows them to make profits from consumers.

What is the best way to contact a credit-reporting company?

The best way to contact credit-reporting agencies is in writing, regardless of what type of request is being made. Furthermore, when sending the letters, consumers should always request return receipt through certified mail. The benefits of doing so are second to none. First and foremost, a return receipt allows you to know that the agency did receive your correspondence. Depending upon the type of request, there are time frames that credit-reporting agencies must adhere to. We will further discuss these in the chapter about disputing items on your credit report. By contacting the agencies in this fashion, consumers are holding them accountable for receiving their documented requests and acting accordingly within legal time frames specified in the Fair Credit Reporting Act. In the unfortunate event that a consumer may have to take legal action against a credit-reporting company, he or she will have a paper trail indicating initial and subsequent contact with the agency. The return receipt will serve as proof that the agency actually received the documents.

For whatever reason, if consumers prefer contacting a credit-reporting agency by telephone, it is imperative that they document every single detail of conversations with representatives. Write down dates, times, names and answers to any questions that you may have asked. Also, if the representative does not summarize the call, ask him or her to do so. Woe is the day that you provide the agency with a list of items that are incorrect and the representative misses one or misinterprets your concern regarding the item! Always make the representative summarize your request. If not, 30 days down the road, you will be livid upon discovering that a concern or two were inadequately addressed or not addressed at all.

It is more difficult to prove what has transpired in a telephone conversation with a credit-reporting company as opposed to proving what has transpired in writing. That is why I recommend contacting agencies in writing whenever possible. Regardless of how you contacted the agency, always follow up. If you have not received a response from the credit-reporting agency within the specified time frame under law (normally 30 calendar days for disputes, 21 days for residents of Maine), send another letter or make a telephone call to check the status. All consumers should request a copy of their credit report at least once a year. You may contact the three major credit-reporting agencies at the following addresses:

Equifax
PO Box 740241
Atlanta, GA 30374
1-800-585-1111

Experian
PO Box 2002
Allen, TX 75013
1-888-397-3742

Trans Union
PO Box 1000
Chester, PA 19022
1-800-916-8800

Chapter summary

The use of credit provides benefits to all of the parties involved in the process and helps to maintain a healthy economy. It's important to note that while utilization of credit is beneficial, consumers must learn not to become dependent on it. This idea alone is the most compelling thought and advice that must be embedded into the minds of all individuals seeking financial independence and success. Thomas J. Stanley, best-selling author of *The Millionaire Next Door* and *The Millionaire Mind*, has conducted extensive research on the behaviors of some of our country's most financially secure citizens. One of the common traits the majority of his subjects identified as contributing to their economic success was the fact that while they utilized credit, they were not dependent on it. Our credit-reporting system relies on the cooperation of multiple groups (or players) to keep it functioning effectively. The players must all serve the critical functions that are necessary to keep the process operating. Knowing the unique responsibilities of the major players and seeing where they fit in the scheme accentuates consumers' comprehension of the entire credit-reporting system. Understanding how to interpret credit reports and obtain them is required of all consumers to ensure they can make informed and intelligent decisions affecting their credit standing.

Now that you have learned the basics of credit, its benefits, the major movers and shakers and all about credit reports, please take a few minutes to test your knowledge on the material. Following is a short quiz that may be used to gauge your understanding of the material as well as reinforce the information that you've acquired. Put your best foot forward and take a stab at it. Good luck!

Chapter 1—Quiz

1. What is credit?

2. Who are the major players in our credit-reporting system?

3. What are the three types of credit accounts?

*** Bonus: Name the three national credit-reporting agencies.

Chapter 1—Quiz Answers

1. Credit is anything of value entrusted to another; it encompasses the idea of receiving now and paying later.

2. There are five major players in our credit-reporting system. They are credit-reporting agencies, furnishers of credit, the Federal Trade Commission (government), consumer credit counselors and consumers.

3. The three types of credit accounts are installment, open and revolving.

*** Bonus: The three national credit-reporting agencies are Experian, Trans Union, and Equifax.

Establishing Credit and Responsibilty

No credit

O ne of the most commonly asked questions by consumers is, "How do I establish credit if I keep getting denied credit?" The truth is, establishing credit for the first time can be accomplished in a number of ways. If a person has attempted to build credit for the first time and has been denied, it is not a good idea to continue applying for credit with various companies. If this pattern of behavior is continued, it will only result in a credit record overflowing with creditor inquiries. This chapter will give you insight to establishing credit for the first time, as well as tell you how to go about reestablishing credit after a financial setback has occurred.

One good way to establish credit is to ask a friend or relative with good credit history to co-sign for or with you on an application. When this happens, the person who already has credit established will share responsibility in some capacity for making sure the account remains in good standing and is paid in a timely manner. The other party's relationship to the account will vary, depending upon whether the account is established as joint/shared or co-sign/comaker. Joint/shared means both parties share equal responsibility for repayment of the debt associated with the account. Co-sign/comaker indicates that one party is primarily responsible for repayment (this person is generally referred to as the "maker" or "primary") however, the other party agrees to assume complete responsibility if the primary borrower defaults.

Regardless of what role you play in the process, it is important to know that your credit history will reflect the other party's payment pattern on the associated account. This means, if one party defaults and becomes delinquent on the debt, the negative rating associated with the late(s) will also be submitted to your credit record.

Some financial advisors have misled consumers into thinking they can obtain another person's credit score by becoming an authorized user on a credit card. This information is simply not true. We'll discuss this more in the credit scoring chapter. But keep in mind that it is wise to exercise extreme caution anytime you may be considering entering into a credit contract with another party, regardless of who the other person is. Many times consumers experience adverse credit ratings at the hands of the ones closest to them, including relatives and loved ones. Be careful!

If you are not able to persuade a friend or relative to co-sign for you, try asking him or her to add you to an existing revolving account·as an authorized user. This method is often the preferred method, because you may enjoy all of the benefits of having a charge card, with minimal responsibility. If you are an authorized user on the account, it means you can charge and make purchases, but are not directly responsible for making the payment to the creditor. The account will also be reported to your credit record, listing you as a user.

If you choose to become an authorized user, you must understand that if the person responsible for making the credit payment defaults, the negative rating will also be reported to your credit history. This technique is still one of choice, however, because even if the negative rating gets attached to your credit record, if you contest the item through the credit-reporting company, most of the time the creditor will expunge the entry from your record because you were only listed as an authorized user. Just know the risk involved in becoming an authorized user. (In this scenario, it is also a good idea to contact the creditor directly and request that the account be removed from your credit record. You may have to submit such a request in writing, but it is definitely worth the time and energy if you can get the negative entry removed from your credit report.)

As a last resort, you may still be able to establish credit by contributing money to fund a credit card's credit line. These are also known as secured credit lines. With these types of accounts, consumers contribute money up front—say $500—that becomes the credit limit on the account. After the credit line has been established, the consumer may use the card in the same manner as an unsecured card, making monthly payments and the like.

To aid in establishing credit, it is a very good idea to have an existing checking or savings account. Most companies will ask this question on the credit application. Having one or both of these accounts helps to ensure that consumers will be able to make payments on the credit card or loan. Before you apply, ask about the company's policy and guidelines for extending credit to customers who are attempting to build credit.

There are some companies who never extend credit to consumers with insufficient credit history. They do not want to take the risk of granting credit to an individual who is unable to prove that he or she has previously handled credit wisely; therefore, they decline the application. You may save yourself some time, and have one less inquiry on your credit record, by asking the right questions before submitting an application.

Don't be fooled by preapproved credit offers either! These marketing letters lead consumers to believe that they will be extended credit upon submitting the completed application to the inquiring company. When you receive one of those letters, the truth is they have received very limited information about you and absolutely nothing specific about your credit history. Promotional offers will be discussed at a later time.

In other instances, first-time applicants with very little or no credit may receive a firm offer, but it has certain restrictions. For example, the applicant may have applied for a credit line of $5,000 but was approved for a credit line of only $1,000. Another example of a restricted offer often occurs with service providers, especially telecommunications and wireless companies.

If limitations are placed on an offer or service, creditors are still required by federal law to send consumers adverse action letters. In these offers, the amount of service made available to a consumer is limited. For example, instead of a consumer being able to make an infinite number of dollars worth of long distance calls, he or she may have a long distance spending limit of $300 or $400. When the spending limit is reached, no additional long distance calls can be dialed until a payment has been received. Other times, a consumer may only be eligible for one phone line as opposed to multiple lines.

My recommendation is for consumers to accept the lesser offer, especially if they have experienced credit problems in the past or have very little credit established. Most creditors are willing to remove service restrictions and/or increase credit limits after a certain amount of consecutive on-time payments have been made. For consumers attempting to build or rebuild their credit, this could present a golden opportunity.

"That account belongs to my ex"

For everyone that has divorced from a spouse, listen carefully. Even if there are accounts listed in a divorce decree to be paid by your spouse, your responsibility for those debts is not absolved. Why? The original agreement you entered into with your spouse and the creditor takes precedence over any subsequent contracts or orders—even issued in court—including divorce decrees. It cannot be superceded and your liability cannot be released unless the creditor agrees to do so. If this ever happens, it would behoove you to send copies of the divorce decree to each of your creditors and request that your name is removed from the debt. If you have good negotiating and persuasive abilities, the creditor may honor that request. Understand, however, that it does not have to, and it probably will not if the debt is in arrears or an adverse standing, especially with a high balance remaining. If a creditor does agree to release you from a debt obligation, make sure you request a letter (on the company's letterhead) indicating such an agreement has been reached. In addition, it is imperative to request that the credit grantor removes the item from your credit report by notifying all credit-reporting agencies.

Applying for and reestablishing credit

So you've had to file for bankruptcy, because you lost that six-figure income. How do you go about reestablishing credit? Once a consumer has experienced major credit setbacks, before he or she begins to reestablish credit, one must understand that the days of receiving 3.5 percent annual percentage rates for credit cards or

1.9 percent auto financing are probably gone for the moment, so don't expect them.

While you may not be able to enjoy the gold or platinum rates offered by some credit card companies, it is still possible to rebuild credit. However, the repercussions of previously defaulting will warrant future creditors to charge higher rates in any offers made. In the meantime it would be wise to hold off on purchasing that brand new European sports car that you've always wanted, unless you wish to pay extremely high finance charges and interest rates for the next three to five years. By the time you own the automobile, you have probably paid the bank two times the value of the car.

If you feel compelled to enter into a loan of any sort during this time put your persuasive skills to work and try to convince someone with an impeccable credit record to co-sign for you. Otherwise, you may look forward to receiving 20-plus percent finance charges for the loan you have decided to accept. Follow the exact same technique if you wish to open a revolving line of credit. Unfortunately, most consumers will not be able to convince a relative or other loved one to enter into a credit obligation with them after experiencing financial difficulties. Instead, this sector may have to settle for the higher interest rates and finance charges, at least for a brief period.

However, did you know that there are a number of businesses that serve and specifically market high-interest credit cards to consumers who are considered "high risk"? In fact, this particular market is very lucrative. Companies serving the high-risk sector reap rewarding profits due, in part, to the outrageous rates they charge (sometimes as high as 35 percent on purchases), the national size of the high-risk audience, as well as the rigorous collection efforts made by aggressive debt recovery employees who traditionally work for them.

Exercise extreme caution when doing business with these types of organizations. If purchases can be made without the use of a credit card, choose that option instead. Doing so will save you money and help ensure that you are on the right track to reestablishing and using credit responsibly. Let's take a closer look at the amount of money a consumer could possibly incur as a result of accepting a high-interest credit card. We'll start by increasing our understanding of how monthly finance charges are calculated. Whether you are fond of math or not, you'll enjoy this, I promise!

Formula for calculating finance charges:

Annual Percentage Rate × One Penny × Avg. Daily Balance × Days in Billing Cycle = total #1.

Divide total #1 by the number of days per year.

Note: the annual percentage rate, average daily balance, and days in a billing cycle are variables.

Valerie's car was repossessed last year while she was laid off. In her efforts to rebuild credit, she applied for and accepted a Champion Classic Visa credit card with an annual percentage rate of 31.9 percent. Valerie purchases a plane ticket to Las Vegas for $275.00 as a gift to herself for landing a new job. Including weekend car rental, hotel, meals, and leisure activities, Val's travel expenses totaled approximately $750.00. Unless Valerie repays this amount in full, she will be charged 31.9 percent on any balance that carries over. If Valerie makes a minimum payment of $15 (bringing her balance to $735) and does not use the credit card again, here is how finance charges will be determined:

$$\text{Finance Charges} = \frac{31.9\% \times .01 \times \$735 \times 28}{365} = \$17.98$$

Champion is truly victorious because they have just earned $17.98 from Valerie's weekend of fun. Furthermore, they will continue to be the champs until the entire balance is paid off. The finance charge of $17.98 will be added to the current amount due ($735.00), making Val's new balance $752.98. Each month Champion will apply 31.9 percent to the existing unpaid balance to assess finance charges. At this rate (paying *the minimum monthly payment), Valerie will only be able to pay for finance charges and never reduce the principal amount of the debt.*

This story was told to illustrate and teach an invaluable lesson: never charge an amount in excess of what you can afford to repay in a single billing cycle—regardless of how low your rates are!

If it is impossible to make a purchase with check or cash, and credit card is the only option available, consumers should make every effort to pay the entire balance in full upon receiving the statement. The bank issuing the credit card usually adds a finance charge to any portion of a balance that remains unpaid, as previously demonstrated. Depending upon how high the annual percentage rate of the credit is, some consumers may find themselves paying monthly finance charges so high that the payments never lower the principal amount of the debt. This is especially true for high interest rate credit cards with large balances. It would be wise for such balances to be transferred to lower interest credit cards if at all possible.

I have known some consumers who are able to obtain low interest loans to pay off high interest credit cards. This is a better idea than continuing to pay on the high interest credit card for a number of reasons.

First, a loan does not require consumers to pay a minimum amount; it will be established in a way such that a constant (unchanging) figure will be due every month. The idea of a minimum amount is the very concept that encourages consumers to allow balances to linger; and as those balances linger, creditors assess finance charges. Don't think creditors are being nice or considerate by offering a "minimum amount"; they have their bottom lines in mind—not necessarily the well-being of their customers. This, too, is the case when an account statement reads "no payment due" or some similar wording, but reflects a balance. This is actually quite a clever idea.

Next, when consumers take out loans, they generally know up front what finance charges are applied to their loans; normally, these charges are not incurred monthly. The finance charges are added during the inception of the loan and included with the principal amount. Finally, because of the structure of this type of credit, consumers can realize and notice visible reductions in the amount of the debt as they make monthly payments. This phenomenon cannot be observed as conspicuously while paying high interest credit cards.

Consumers who can successfully transfer or pay off high interest credit card balances should contact the creditor with the high interest and ask for a lower rate. Often creditors will lower their rates for customers when asked to do so, especially if the customer is loyal and has performed well in the past. Do not hesitate to request a more competitive rate, particularly if all or the last several payments have been made on time. If the creditor does not lower the rate, suggest closing the account. I have personally used this technique successfully. Creditors do not like losing business and a good one will offer options, or at least negotiate, to keep good customers. Always try to barter for better rates prior to closing an account, but let the credit grantor know that you're serious about your intentions and will have no regrets about ending the business relationship.

Applying for credit

Occasionally, credit grantors will have to manually review applications for credit. A manual review may be warranted for a number of reasons. When attempting to perform a credit check, the credit-reporting company may be unable to return a credit score. Inability to receive a credit score is generally triggered by the lack of a needed credit file attribute or the presence of a characteristic preventing the scoring model/software from generating a numeric value. Another factor that may result in manual review is the presence of a fraud alert on the credit file. In such cases, a creditor may have a department of associates that will request additional information from the applicant. Normally, these employees will ask probing questions regarding the consumer's credit history that only he or she should know. The employee will peruse the consumer's credit record and proceed with interrogating the applicant. Some examples of questions asked may include: "Can you verify your full name, date of birth and Social Security number?" "Do you currently have or have you previously had any major credit cards, and if so, what is the name of the issuer?" "Have you ever had an auto loan, and if so, who financed the vehicle?" "Can you give me the name of a current or previous employer?"

In most cases this process is merely an extra precaution taken to protect the identity of the applicant. Would you be able to answer any of the questions listed if a creditor presented them to you? It has been my experience working for a credit-reporting agency and service provider alike, that many consumers are oblivious about the content of their credit records. Believe it or not, consumers may be denied credit based upon the fact that they cannot verify information appearing on their credit reports, even if there are no negative marks listed. Thus, it is equally important that consumers are aware of the content of their credit reports before submitting applications for credit or even before applying for credit by telephone.

What about consumer statements?

Consumers may add a statement to their credit records to serve as an explanation for certain items on their credit reports. For example, Jane Consumer wishes to add a consumer statement to her credit report that explains why she filed for bankruptcy two years ago. The statement is available to any creditors who may review Jane's credit record.

Although consumer statements were designed to allow consumers to shed light on disputed credit entries (those items that have been reverified by a credit-reporting agency and not resolved to a consumer's satisfaction), many use them as a tool to clarify less than favorable information that is accurately appearing on their credit records.

The million-dollar question is: Does adding a consumer statement to a credit report help? Do credit grantors look at them? It has been my experience that creditors rarely allow a consumer statement to influence their decisions to extend and offer or deny an application for credit. For the most part, credit grantors rely on the scoring summary to determine an applicant's eligibility for credit or a service. As credit scoring is systemic, it certainly does not consider a consumer statement nor has does it have the intelligence required to correctly interpret a consumer statement. Reviewing a consumer statement is a manual process and it is more time-consuming. It is possible, though not common, for credit grantors to override systemic credit scoring decisions. Understand that we live in an age of speed and efficiency and that most businesses incorporate techniques to eliminate or at least significantly reduce manual processes. Unless an applicant can convince a creditor to manually review his or her credit record, a consumer statement is of little value.

Reestablishing credit

Consumers wishing to reestablish credit may follow the same guidelines previously discussed for those who have no credit:

- Locate a reputable, creditworthy cosigner.

- Become an authorized user on an account of a consumer with flawless credit.

- Seek a secured loan/credit card from a creditor who reports to credit-reporting agencies.

Don't be misled by advertisements on television and radio that attempt to lure consumers by claiming bankruptcies, foreclosures, liens and other adverse debts will not prevent them from obtaining credit. The truth is, while the presence of delinquencies may not prevent consumers from receiving credit, they may result in painfully high finance charges and interest rates. Not many consumers would rush to auto dealers if they knew they would be charged excessive fees for having poor credit. However, wishful consumers parade out to dealers because deceptive ads appear to be offering a great deal, even if they have previous credit problems. Knowing the right questions to ask may prevent consumers from being suckered into a bad deal. Asking the following question could save time and money:

"If I have experienced past credit problems (you may need to site specific examples), what range of financing am I eligible for?"

Nine times out of 10, the salesperson is going to reply: "I would need to run your credit report before determining what we can offer you." Agreeing to a proposition like this is a mistake. A creditor does not need to access a consumer's credit record to provide a general range of rates available. In fact, creditors—regardless of a consumer's credit standing—predetermine these ranges. Depending upon supply, demand and several other factors, rates being offered will vary. One month the best rate may be 3.9 percent; another it may be 8.9 percent.

Before a consumer gives any merchant permission to review their credit records, he or she should obtain a copy for themselves so that they are aware of the content. Prior to submitting any major application of credit, it is imperative to be cognizant of what is included in one's credit record. The benefits of being aware are immeasurable.

Unfortunately, most consumers do not become aware of errors on their credit reports until after they have applied for credit and have gotten declined. Woe is the day that a consumer applies for credit and gets denied based upon an inaccurate credit report! Knowing the content of one's credit report prior to seeking credit helps to ensure a smoother application process. If mistakes are present, a consumer can resolve them before submitting an application, bypassing the humiliation of being told his or her request has not been approved. Some consumers even discover that they are victims of fraud upon receiving a disclosure of their credit records! When requesting a disclosure of one's credit record, remember to obtain copies from all three national, major credit-reporting agencies.

Avoid unforeseen delays by being well-informed of your credit record. Ask the creditor with which you are considering applying to describe their guidelines for extending credit. Find out what their specific criteria is before completing application paperwork. More detailed questions to pose are:

1. Is there an average length of time (in years) that you require potential applicants to have established? If so, what is it?

2. What type of previous credit (revolving, installments) should a successful applicant be able to show responsible use of?

3. Do you have a score cutoff? If so, what is it?

4. What weight do non-credit-related factors carry in the decision process (such as current income, length of time on current job, length of time at present address, etc.)?

Be especially mindful of auto dealers when car shopping. After visiting one car lot, a consumer could end up with several credit inquiries on his or her credit report. While a consumer is out test-driving a car, the dealer is usually contacting several banks and financing institutions to get a loan approved. Test-driving a car does not allow an auto dealer to sufficiently justify accessing a consumer's credit report, if written or verbal authorization has not been provided. The car-shopping public should not provide auto dealers with their identification unless they are seriously considering making a purchase. Even though inquiries do not have a substantial impact on a consumer's ability to obtain credit, unnecessary accumulation of them creates long, messy credit records.

Do not feel reluctant to ask potential creditors probing questions about their credit extension process. Consumers may measure the authenticity of a merchant's intentions based upon how willing the company is to entertain their preliminary questions. Remember to ask the questions before completing any paperwork or giving verbal consent to a creditor to access your credit record. Making sure that one's credit report is correct prior to requesting credit guarantees a less tedious, embarrassing and bumpy process. Being apprised of one's credit and understanding how to interpret the information allows a consumer to accurately assess the status of his or her overall credit rating and help him or her determine how it may affect his or her ability to be approved on future applications. Thanks to technology and credit-reporting agencies' hungry interests in turning profits, consumers can even receive their credit scores without applying for credit.

It's important to note that consumers should be more concerned with the accuracy of information appearing on their credit reports, as opposed to trying to find ways to increase their credit scores. Focusing on the credit score is not the key to establishing or reestablishing credit. Remember, the credit score is driven directly by the information on a credit report.

Chapter summary

A consumer's lack of knowledge could be a creditor's opportunity to leverage dominance in credit-related matters. It is a power tactic to take advantage of another person's ignorance or lack of understanding. If you are reading this book, you are not a clodhopper, which already sets you apart from many. Credit knowledge will help position consumers on equal playing grounds as lenders. A consumer's ability and technique in applying what credit knowledge he or she has will allow him or her to negotiate terms, rates and more on any contract presented by a creditor. It offers bargaining power, and if a creditor fails to meet one's expectations, he or she should be prepared to take their money and business elsewhere. Let the creditor know this up front!

Ultimately, this knowledge empowers consumers to make sound credit decisions and helps to pave the path to healthier financial futures. Every offer is negotiable. In fact, everything is negotiable, but it is left to the parties involved (creditors and consumers) to decide if they are willing to compromise and establish harmonious relationships.

Consumers should always ask for a better bargain, especially if proper management of financial obligations has been consistently displayed! Why accept an automobile loan at 10.7 percent, even if this is the best rate currently being offered, when your credit history shows that you have been mature and responsible with all of your financial obligations? Most shoppers concede because they find themselves in uncontrollable and untimely situations that demand an immediate resolution. I've done it, and I'm sure you have or have been tempted at some point in your life. Our priorities have to change. Most of us want "it" and we want "it" now!

If your automobile left you stranded, taking public transportation for a month or two is well worth the sacrifice. It is better that you take the time to conduct research and get your credit in order than run hastily to an automobile dealer seeking "help." Lenders know this and indirectly manipulate this type of consumer frequently;

they can identify a buyer's sense of urgency right away. Ask for the better deal or be prepared to leave, and never reveal to any lender that an offer is time sensitive or urgent. Remember, you are in control—no more raw deals! Now, go out and get yourself some credit!

I encourage you to challenge yourself by answering the following quiz. You will never be bullied by an auto salesperson again, and you may be able to get your hopeless son-in-law out of your worries by helping him reestablish his own credit.

Chapter 2—Quiz

1. List one way to establish credit.

2. Preapproval letters are firm offers of credit. (True/False)

3. Does a divorce decree absolve one party from responsibility of a joint debt?

4. How might a person go about reestablishing credit?

5. List two questions to ask a creditor prior to completing an application for credit.

6. Using the formula you've learned for calculating finance charges, if Val pays $25 toward the new balance of $752.98, what will the finance charges be on her upcoming statement? (Assume there are 26 days in the billing cycle.)

Chapter 2—Quiz Answers

1. One way to establish credit is by obtaining a cosigner or becoming an authorized user on an established account (these answers are not all-inclusive).

2. False. Preapproved applications are not firm offers of credit.

3. A divorce decree does not absolve a person from any liability related to a joint debt.

4. A person may reestablish credit by obtaining a cosigner or a secured credit card (these answers are not all-inclusive).

5. Two questions to ask prior to applying for credit are:
   "What criteria does the creditor have for approving credit?"
   and
   "What are the current rates being offered?"

6. $\dfrac{31.9 \times .01 \times 752.98 \times 26}{365} = \$17.11$

Chapter 3

Credit Reports

Ordering a copy of your credit report

Many consumers are unaware of how to obtain a copy of their credit reports. To make matters even worse, many more are unaware that they may be entitled to a free copy from the three credit-reporting agencies (Equifax, Experian and Trans Union). Let's tackle these two issues individually.

First, if a consumer has applied for a credit or benefit and has been denied or has had restrictions placed on an offer, the company making the credit decision (the credit grantor) is required by federal law to provide him or her with the following information in writing:

1. The creditor must inform the consumer that he or she is entitled to a free credit report within 60 days of denial.

2. The name of the credit-reporting agency that furnished the credit report.

3. Specific reason(s) for denial or limitations of credit. Some examples are amount owed on accounts is too high, not enough revolving credit, recent delinquencies reported on accounts, insufficient credit history, and so on.

It is important to understand that the credit-reporting agency that furnished the creditor with the report cannot tell a consumer why he or she may have been denied credit. That responsibility belongs completely to the creditor. This is one of the biggest misconceptions that consumers have about credit-reporting agencies. From this day forward, you know the truth about denial of credit.

The declination letter will contain an address and telephone number to order a credit report from the appropriate agency. The Fair and Accurate Credit Transactions Act of 2003 allows all consumers to receive one free copy of their credit report per year. Beginning December 2004, this federal mandate swept the country in phases, beginning with the western states. For more information about obtaining your free, annual credit report, visit *www.annualcreditreport.com* or call toll-free 1-877-322-8228. There are some states where laws allow its residents to receive free credit reports prior to the amendment by the Fair and Accurate Credit Transactions Act, regardless of whether or not a consumer was denied credit or benefit. Those states are:

+   New Jersey

+   Colorado

- Vermont

- Georgia (residents of Georgia may receive two free credit reports per year)

- Massachusetts

- Maryland

Other states have discounted rates for its residents to receive credit reports if they have not been denied. They are:

- Minnesota—$3; subsequent requests within 12 months are $9

- Maine—$3

- Connecticut—$5

- California—$8

Note: Please be sure to check with the major credit-reporting agencies for the most recent state charges, as they are subject to change depending on state-initiated legislation.

The Fair Credit Reporting Act is a federal body of law that outlines the guidelines that credit-reporting agencies, creditors, debt-management companies and collection agencies must follow to ensure fair treatment to consumers as it relates to credit reporting. The Fair Credit Reporting Act will be discussed in an upcoming chapter. However, at this time we will refer to the portion that relates to receiving disclosure of one's credit history.

Under this body of law, consumers meeting the following criteria are also entitled to a free copy of their credit reports:

- Those receiving welfare or public assistance.

- Those who are unemployed and seeking employment.

- Those who believe their credit record contains fraudulent data.

+ Those consumers requesting their first annual copy.

Any consumers who do not fall into one of the aforementioned categories may be charged a fee of $9.00 to receive a copy of their credit report.

Contacting a credit-reporting agency

Credit-reporting agencies are not required by law to speak to consumers over the telephone unless the consumer possesses a copy of a credit report. I will explain this further, as it may be a bit confusing at first. Let's take a look at an example.

Joe applies for credit at ABC Retail Shop and his application is declined. He receives a letter in the mail four days later advising that Trans Union is the credit-reporting company that furnished ABC Retail Shop with his credit record.

First, Trans Union is the only credit-reporting company that supplied the information to Abc Retail, so he should contact it to receive a free credit report. Even though Equifax and Experian did not provide ABC Retail Shop with Joe's credit report, he should still contact them, but make them secondary on his list. If Joe has already received his free annual credit reports from Experian and Equifax, those two agencies may charge him a fee for the subsequent request (remember, Trans Union's report was the only one reviewed by ABC Retail).

Next, as mentioned earlier, the declination letter will contain an address and telephone number for contacting the appropriate credit-reporting company. The telephone number provided on the letter will not allow Joe to speak with a warm, live body. This number will merely allow him to order a copy of his credit report through an automated system. If the information entered by Joe (via telephone) differs from what the credit-reporting company has in its records (such as his mailing address or Social Security number), Joe will be required to submit his request in writing, along with photocopies of his identification and address. As frustrating as it may seem, this procedure was implemented to aid in the prevention of someone else obtaining access to Joe's personal information; thus, it helps curtail fraud and identity theft.

Once Joe has received a physical copy of the credit report, exclusively from the agency, there will be a telephone number provided for him to call to speak to a live person.

This example outlines the standard practice followed by all three of the national, major credit-reporting companies. Exceptions may apply if consumers have been victims of fraud or have purchased a merged credit report (containing information from all three reporting agencies) offered by a third-party supplier through a business venture with all three credit-reporting agencies. In some cases, credit-reporting companies will allow these individuals to speak to a live person without having a real credit report in their possession.

What type of information does a credit report contain?

Typically, credit reports contain five main types of information. The type of information and how it is reported may vary from agency to agency, but is basically interpreted the same way. Credit-reporting companies obtain all of their information from creditors and furnishers that subscribe to their services. Receiving incorrect or incomplete information from furnishers results in credit agencies listing erroneous data in consumer credit reports.

Each time you complete an application or establish an account with a merchant, the information you provided is taken from the application and reported to credit-reporting companies. Therefore, if there is a mistake listed on your application, or if the creditor enters the data incorrectly, it could result in erroneous information appearing on your credit report. Have you ever received a copy of a credit report with employment listed that is so outdated you cannot even remember working for the company? This would be a prime example of outdated, incorrect information.

Section 1—identification

This section contains items such as name, Social Security number, date of birth, addresses, driver's license numbers, former names and employment information.

Section 2—general accounts

This section refers to the three types of accounts that were previously discussed: open, revolving and installment. It contains credit cards, loans, utilities and the like. As you continue to pay these items, creditors will submit updates to the credit-reporting agencies. Therefore, the information should change periodically (monthly or bimonthly), unless the item(s) are inactive, in which case, it simply reads "inactive" or a similar statement such as "contact creditor for status." These types of accounts (inactive, etc.) neither help nor harm a consumer's credit report (or score).

Section 3—inquiries

Inquiries are requests for a consumer's credit record from various institutions. They may include state and federal agencies, banks, finance companies, department stores, auto dealers, credit card companies, utility companies, employers, and the list goes on and on. Often they are categorized as "hard" and "soft"—"hard" indicating they have an effect on a credit score, and "soft" meaning they do not.

Section 4—collection agency accounts

Debts that have been referred to collection companies for recovery will appear in this portion of a credit report.

Section 5—public records

This section contains items that are recorded in local, state and federal courts. Courts do not report public record data to credit-reporting companies. The credit-reporting companies may have established relationships with vendors that are charged with retrieving this type of information from various courts throughout the country. When the data is retrieved, it is placed on the appropriate credit record, as it is believed to be an indication of a consumer's payment history. For the longest time, it was difficult for vendors to verify court records (for re-verification requests) because of antedated retrieval procedures. Fortunately, many of the courts are able to verify public record information electronically, much like larger credit grantors.

While the completeness of each credit-reporting agency's credit report may vary for each of these sections, they will all contain these five components. For example, one major reporting company reports consumers' driver's license numbers in the identification section, but the others do not. Regardless of this difference, they all produce reports with an identification section. Understand that the amount of identification information may vary.

Retention of information on credit reports

Prior to consumers applying for and accepting credit, they should know how long the debt may remain on their credit records. Whether the debt remains in good or poor standing throughout its lifetime, it will become a part of a consumer's credit history. Also, before contacting a credit-reporting company with a dispute on a credit file, consumers should know how long entries might be retained under state and federal laws. This section will discuss retention of various entries that commonly appear on consumer credit reports.

Many consumers inundate credit-reporting agencies with erroneous requests for re-verification concerning the length of time an item has been appearing on their credit reports. (The most common request is for a negative entry to be deleted because it's been reporting for more than seven years from the date it was originally opened). There is an even greater number of consumers who apply for credit every day not knowing what appears on their credit records.

Entries appearing on credit reports contain multiple dates (open dates, report dates, status dates, last payment dates, and so on). It's paramount for consumers to know which dates to use in calculating the amount of time an entry may appear on their credit records. As previously discussed, there are some states with special laws allowing different time frames for credit entries to be expunged. These unique state laws must be honored by credit-reporting agencies as long as they do not conflict with federal laws. We will now focus on understanding how long various items can be retained on consumer credit reports as specified under state and federal laws. Let's take a more detailed look at basic retention of credit data.

General accounts (open, installment and revolving) remain on credit records for seven to 10 years from the date of last activity—not from the opened date! The date of last activity could mean a number of things. It could mean:

1. The date on which the account was last used (charged on).

2. The date on which the last payment was made.

3. The date on which the account was closed.

4. The date on which the account went into a delinquency status and never recovered or regained a current status (such as the date the account was charged off, went to collections, and so on).

Once an account has been charged off or has reached a collection status, the creditor(s) cannot change the date of last activity, even if, subsequently, a consumer makes a payment or the creditor sells or transfers the debt to another company such as a collection agency. The date of last activity cannot change. If a creditor does alter the date of last activity in this fashion, it is violating the Fair Credit Reporting Act and is opening itself up to litigation from consumers and complaints to the Federal Trade Commission, which could possibly result in costly fines.

To determine, specifically, how long a general account will remain on a consumer's credit record, the relevant factors that he or she must consider are the dates of last activity and the rating of the account at the time it was last active. For example:

Emma has two accounts appearing on her credit record. One is a Tire & Car Care credit card that has been charged off. It shows a date of last activity of 10/03. The other is an XYZ Bank auto loan that has been paid and never been late. It shows a date of last activity of 12/04.

Because the Tire & Car Care account has a negative rating, it will be removed seven years from the date of last activity, which is 10/2010. Negative items (commonly called adverse items) are purged seven years from the date of last activity. Under the Fair Credit Reporting Act, these type items cannot remain on credit records for more than seven years from the last activity date. New York residents have special state laws for paid charge-offs and repossessions; they cannot remain longer than five years from the date of last activity. The XYZ bank account does not reflect a negative status. Therefore, it could remain on the credit file for up to 10 years from the last activity date, which is 12/2014.

Under the Fair Credit Reporting Act, general accounts that are in good-standing can remain for up to 10 years from the date of last activity, depending upon the credit-reporting agency's discretion, as long as they are not violating the statute of limitations under the Fair Credit Reporting Act. Thus, one credit-reporting company may keep the good standing item on a consumer's credit record for seven years from the date of last activity and another may keep it for 10 years. If it is a positive account, it does not hurt consumers if the item remains on his or her credit record for 10 years. In fact, it is always good to show positive payment history on a credit report. It's a good idea to leave accounts showing positive ratings alone. Woe is the day a consumer disputes one, and 30 days later it is deleted from his or her credit report because the creditor did not respond to the re-verification request or instructed the reporting agency to remove the item. In this case, a perfectly good-standing account reflecting positive repayment history has been removed from the credit report. Further, it could have an unfavorable impact on a consumer's credit score. Credit scoring and the impact of adding and remov-ing·entries will be addressed in a future chapter.

Collection agency accounts remain on credit records for a maximum of seven years from the date of last activity. Remember, these are debts that originated with one creditor or company but have been sold to another business to offset losses or outsourced for recovery of payment. It's important to note that even if a debt has been sold, the date of last activity cannot be changed. In the state of New York, paid collection agency items can remain a maximum of five years from the date of last activity. This law only applies to consumers who are current residents of New York, not those who were born there and moved to another state. Conversely, consumers who were born or previously resided in another state may reap the rewards of this law upon becoming official residents of New York.

At the time of this writing, New York is the only state that has special laws regarding the retention of collection items on credit reports. I hope this does not encourage everyone in other states (who have a few credit concerns) to close shop and move to the Big Apple!

Public record items such as liens, garnishments, bankruptcies, and judgments, remain on credit records for seven to 10 years from their filing dates (in most states). The filing date is the date in which a public record item is recorded in court. Let's take a closer look at the retention of public record items individually.

Liens

For residents of all states other than California, unpaid liens may remain on credit records indefinitely. Yes, indefinitely! The government (local, state and federal) wants its money. If liens are paid, they may remain on credit records for seven years from the date paid/released. The term "released" means "paid" for tax liens. Again, how long a credit-reporting company chooses to retain liens may vary, as long as the previous law is not violated.

Keep in mind that the government—at any level—does not issue directives to credit-reporting agencies to attach public record items to credit records; the agencies are proactive in gathering and attaching this information. In the state of California, paid or unpaid liens may remain on credit records for no more than 10 years from the date filed. At the time of this writing, California is the only state with special laws concerning the retention of liens.

Garnishments

Garnishments are filed to take a portion of a consumer's wages for repayment of a debt owed to a creditor or other party. They may be retained on credit reports no more than seven years from the dates they are filed. Currently, no special state laws or exceptions apply to the retention of garnishments on credit files.

Judgments

Judgments are debt obligations to creditors resulting from court orders or decrees. They remain on credit records for seven years, whether they have been satisfied (paid) or not. At the present time, the only exception is for residents of New York, where judgments that have been satisfied are deleted from credit records five years from the filing date.

Bankruptcies

Most credit records will list two types of bankruptcies: Chapter 7 and Chapter 13. Sometimes credit reports may include Chapter 11 and 12 bankruptcies as well. Let's define and determine the retention of them.

The key difference between a Chapter 7 and Chapter 13 bankruptcy is that the Chapter 7 may allow a consumer to be exonerated from debts owed to creditors, meaning settlements may be accepted—but not necessarily full payments—and in most cases, creditors do not receive anything. If a consumer is exonerated from his or her debts, the Chapter 7 is considered discharged. In this case, normally a consumer's assets are liquidated and creditors are paid at least a portion of the amount due to them.

On the other hand, a Chapter 13 bankruptcy allows a consumer to fulfill debts owed to creditors through a repayment plan. The repayment plan, which is established through bankruptcy court and supervised by a trustee, is also known as a wage earner plan. A portion of a consumer's wages is deducted and distributed to creditors until the debt(s) are repaid in full. Under a Chapter 13, when all debts have been paid in full, the bankruptcy is considered discharged.

Chapter 11 bankruptcies are normally filed by businesses, but may be filed by individuals as well. This type of bankruptcy allows an individual or company to reorganize its finances while continuing to conduct business. If you've ever wondered how so many big-name corporations are able to remain in business after filing bankruptcy, it's probably because they filed Chapter 11. During the reorganization period, the goal of the business is to stimulate its resources and reap profits. Under a Chapter 11, all major decisions that could potentially affect the profitability of the company must receive the court's approval.

Chapter 12 bankruptcies are filed by farmers or sharecroppers who are experiencing severe financial difficulties. In much the same way a Chapter 11 bankruptcy allows reorganization of finances, so does a Chapter 12. It allows farmers to retain their farms, as they are the primary or only source of income, and complete a repayment plan to fulfill debt obligations to creditors.

There is a compelling need for consumers to understand the difference between "discharged" and "dismissed" Chapter 7 and 13 bankruptcies. Because these two bankruptcies are the two filed primarily by consumers, our discussion about disposition (dismissed and discharged) will pertain to them. Now that you understand how the term "discharged" is applied to these types of bankruptcies, we will focus our attention on "dismissed." A dismissed filing could also mean that a consumer (through a bankruptcy court and with an appointed trustee) filed the appropriate documents to start bankruptcy proceedings but decided to withdraw. In other words, a consumer may have decided to stop any further proceedings after the initial paperwork to begin the process has already been submitted to a bankruptcy court. A Chapter 13 bankruptcy may also be dismissed if the filer or his employer fails to make payments as prescribed under the wage-earner agreement. In either case, the bankruptcy may still appear on a consumer's credit report for up to 10 years from the original filing date.

What most consumers fail to understand is that a dismissed bankruptcy will remain on their credit records, even if they decide to discontinue the process in the middle of proceedings. For the record, dismissed bankruptcies are just as eligible as discharged bankruptcies to be attached to credit reports.

A new bill has been introduced in Congress that will change the way Chapter 7 bankruptcies are filed. Once enacted, the bill would essentially make it more difficult for consumers to be exonerated from debts. Supported by a host of retailers, credit card companies and banks, the bill would allow a consumer's income to be a factor considered when determining eligibility for filing a Chapter 7 bankruptcy. Consumers whose annual incomes meet or exceed a state's average income (this is determined by census figures in the state where a consumer resides) and have at least $100 dollars of disposable income available per month would be forced to repay their debts through a Chapter 13 bankruptcy. The bankruptcy bill would also require filers to enroll in credit counseling at their own expense.

Despite record levels of profitability from consumer lending, supporters of the bill contend that such changes are needed to offset losses caused by consumers who file Chapter 7 bankruptcies. On the other hand, opponents argue that the bill would encourage credit card issuers, particularly, to expand the number of consumers that are eligible for credit. Basically, by tightening the rules of filing Chapter 7 bankruptcies and forcing more consumers to repay debts, the risks associated with lending to consumers decreases and creditors have a better chance of being paid. As a result, opponents believe consumers who have less than perfect credit will be inundated with more credit offers.

Now, let's talk retention! Chapter 7 and 13 bankruptcies that are dismissed may remain on credit records for 10 years from the date filed. No special state laws exist that may decrease this time frame. Chapter 7 bankruptcies that have been discharged remain on credit reports for 10 years from the filing dates and Chapter 13 bankruptcies that have been discharged remain for seven years from their filing dates. Sometimes Chapter 11 bankruptcies (for businesses) and Chapter 12 bankruptcies (for farmers and sharecroppers) may appear on credit records. They each may be retained for seven years from the filing dates, regardless of their disposition. Disposition refers to the status of a bankruptcy (dismissed, discharged, pending).

Chapter summary

Being knowledgeable about retention and knowing the content of one's credit record helps eliminate unexpected surprises that many consumers face when submitting new applications for credit. The Fair and Accurate Transactions Act allows every consumer to receive at least one free disclosure of his or her credit report annually.

Due to this enactment and many other advancements executed to ease the disclosure process for consumers, there is no valid excuse for anyone to be unaware of the content of his or her credit file. Failure to take advantage of this awesome benefit would be a tragedy and disservice to many consumer advocates and similar organizations that have dedicated tremendous efforts to increasing consumer access to their own information. Knowing how long various entries may be retained on consumer credit reports allows consumers to accurately predict short- and long-term effects of debt obligations, whether they have defaulted or paid the debt as agreed. Further, because proper retention expectations would have been determined previously, when they contact the credit-reporting agencies, they will optimize their time by only contesting erroneous items.

Consumers will be in positions to identify and challenge any inappropriate alterations of dates that will allow adverse entries to remain on their credit files longer than state and federal law warrants.

At the end of this chapter you will find a chart that may be used as a retention reference guide. As state laws constantly change, it is best to contact your state legislative office to verify the most current, accurate retention rules. For those of you on the expert track, a quiz follows to validate your understanding of credit reports and data retention. All others may proceed to the next section. Keep reading!

Chapter 3—Quiz

1. What three pieces of information must every declination letter include?

2. What is the price of a credit report, assuming that one has not been denied credit?

3. What are the five main sections of all credit reports?

4. What is the "date of last activity" or "last activity date"?

5. How long may a dismissed Chapter 13 bankruptcy appear on a credit record?

6. How long may late payments on accounts appear on credit records?

7. How long may an unpaid lien remain on a credit record?

8. How long do creditor inquiries usually remain on credit records?

*** Bonus: Federal retention laws always dictate how long an item may remain on a credit record (True/Flase).

Chapter 3—Quiz Answers

1. Every declination letter must contain a statement that a consumer is entitled to a free credit report within 60 days of being denied credit, reason(s) for denial or a note that the reasons may be obtained upon requesting them and the name of the credit-reporting agency used in making the credit decision.

2. The cost of a credit report is $9.00 (given a consumer is not entitled to receive one free of charge) for most states, with some states having special, reduced rates.

3. The five main sections of a credit report are identification, inquiries, public record, collection and general accounts.

4. The "date of last activity" is the original date of delinquency for an account that never recovered—the date of the last payment/transaction.

5. A dismissed Chapter 13 bankruptcy may appear on a credit record for 10 years from the filing date.

6. Late payments on accounts may appear on a credit record for seven years from the date of occurrence.

7. Unpaid liens may appear on credit records indefinitely, except for residents of California.

8. Inquiries usually remain on credit records for one to two years.

*** Bonus: False. State laws may override federal laws as long as they do not conflict.

Retention Rules

Credit Item	Maximum Federal Retention Rule	Maximum State Retention Rule
Chapter 13 Bankruptcy	10 years from date filed	Not applicable
Chapter 12 Bankruptcy	10 years from date filed	Not applicable
Chapter 7 Bankruptcy	10 years from date filed	Not applicable
Civil Suit	Seven years from date filed	Not applicable
Civil Judgment	Seven years from date filed	N.Y.—five years from date filed (if satisfied)
Paid Tax Lien	Seven years from the date of payment	Calif.—10 years from date filed
Unpaid Tax Lien	Not specified by federal law	Calif.—10 years from date filed
Collection Account	Seven years from the original delinquency date	N.Y.—five years from the original delinquency date (if paid)
Charge-Offs and Repossessions	Seven years from the original delinquency date	N.Y.—five years from the original delinquency date (if paid)
Late Payments	Seven years from the date of occurrence	Not applicable
Employment Inquiries	Two years from the date of inquiry	Not applicable
All other Inquiries	One year from the date of inquiry	Not applicable

Establishing Utility Services Using Credit

Overcoming utility service hurdles

The objective of this chapter is to tell you how your credit is used in establishing utility services and to prepare you for identity verification hurdles you may have to jump during the process. Many utility and telecommunication service providers use access to credit-reporting agencies' databases to assist them in making credit decisions. Consumers who are denied credit are often perplexed about not being able to establish basic services such as electricity, gas, cable, or even telephone. They are even more astonished to learn that their credit reports could prevent them from receiving a service and/or warrant the provider in taking adverse action. If not entirely declined, a provider may place restrictions on the service such as offering one telephone line, as opposed to multiple lines requested by a consumer or business; limiting a telephone offer to local service only; limiting the amount of long distance usage (in dollars or minutes available); and with some wireless communication providers, phone and other equipment purchases may have to be placed on a credit card, as oppose to being billed to the account.

Another method service providers use in lowering risk with consumers defaulting is to require a security deposit be paid prior to the service being established. The amount of a deposit may vary, depending upon how poor a consumer's credit history is. Some services, such as cellular, may require deposits as much as a couple hundred dollars— or more, in worst-case scenarios. Consumers asked to pay large deposits for mobile phones may opt to use prepaid cellular services, but for general household essentials, such as gas and electricity, alternative options are limited. Fortunately, most deposits required for household utilities are not as burdensome as those of cellular services.

In addition to using credit reports to help make sound business decisions, service providers may access another separate database managed or owned by consumer-reporting agencies. These repositories are completely independent from the database used to store consumer credit reports. They may be regional or national in terms of the geographical area covered. For example, service providers wishing to broadly investigate unpaid utility and telecommunication debts may have access to a national repository. On the other hand, providers primarily interested in regional unpaid debts may only access regional databases. In the event that a service provider locates an unpaid debt in one of the databases, the service may be denied or limited. These databases are referred to as "exchanges." They are often owned or managed by major credit-reporting agencies and usually consist of unpaid utility and telecommunication accounts of consumers. Various service providers that are contributing members to the database report the debts. Once a delinquent bill has been paid, it is either updated to reflect a zero balance or expunged from the database. Exchanges may exist for individual consumers as well as businesses, but the data is separate, meaning delinquent business accounts are not stored in the same medium as delinquent consumer accounts. More cautious providers may view a consumer's credit report in addition to conducting a search for an unpaid utility or telephone bill. Consumers owing an unpaid debt located in one of the regional or national databases will be instructed to contact the consumer-reporting agency that has the listing in its records. Upon contact, a consumer will receive a live representative that will verbally disclose the debt and follow up by sending a hard copy of the bill to the consumer. If a provider's decision was only based on review of a consumer credit report, he or she will receive a general summary of items appearing on the report that contributed to denial of service or another adverse action. Because of the necessity of these services, a consumer who has been denied a utility or telecommunication service has access to a live associate at the reporting agency; however, consumers denied other types of credit do not have the luxury of reaching a live body until after they have received a copy of the agency's report.

There are also times when a consumer's request for a utility or other service is not granted based upon an identification discrepancy. Providers also use credit reports to help confirm the identity of applicants. There are some clever consumers who attempt to use the names and Social Security numbers of minors (particularly their children) to establish utility services. Make no mistake, this is indeed identity theft, but it occurs more often than one can ever imagine. Other consumers will attempt to use a combination of identities such as their names and their childrens' Social Security numbers to establish services. Neither of these deceptive ploys is usually successful. As a tool in deterring fraud, a credit-reporting agency may often be able to determine the year in which a Social Security number was issued and, in turn, convey that information to the service provider. Therefore, a skilled and attentive provider will be alarmed if an adult applying for services has a Social Security number that has been issued only a few years ago. There are some exceptions to this scenario, such as immigrants who have recently obtained citizenship and Social Security numbers. In this situation, an adult consumer is going to have a fairly new Social Security number in terms of the date it was issued. The individual may have to provide the utility or telecommunication company with proof of identity, in person, and explain that he or she is a new citizen in the United States with a recently issued Social Security number.

Credit-reporting agencies now offer identity authentication products to many service providers, especially those in the wireless communications industry. As noted in the fraud and identify theft section of this book, the frequency of credit fraud and identity theft in this sector continues to proliferate, particularly with the establishment of new accounts. These identity authentication products analyze new applications and measure them against certain attributes related to fraud. The basis for detecting fraud usually derives from huge fraud databases that various industries (credit cards, retailers, auto loans, etc.) contribute data to. The contributors load the database with certain characteristics and alerts of confirmed fraud as discovered on their applications. If warranted, the fraud detection product may suggest manual review of an application by a breathing body, in which case the employee of the service provider will ask the applicant a series of probing questions pertaining to his or her credit report. The employee will ask the applicant to verify all of his or her identity (complete name, Social Security number, date of birth) and current and previous addresses. In some cases, the employee will ask about current and former employment (which is useless in verifying identity because employment is frequently inaccurate on credit reports) and questions regarding past and current credit obligations (such as credit cards, department store cards, mortgage loans, auto loans, student loans, and even inquiries). If the applicant correctly answers a certain number of questions, his or her identity is considered verified and the application will be approved; however, if the applicant fails to correctly or completely answer the questions, the application will be declined and the consumer will be referred to the appropriate credit-reporting agency to obtain a copy of his or her credit report. This unique and helpful process is a way for creditors and service providers to proactively curtail the likelihood of fraud and identity theft in their industries. Many of them have significantly decreased losses due to fraud by investing in fraud detection and automated identity authentication systems.

Establishing utility and telecommunication services may also be impacted by non-credit-related factors. The service provider may assess deposits based upon an applicant's lack of experience in paying for a like service. For example, if an applicant has never had gas services activated in his name, a deposit may be required. Usually, if a deposit is required for this reason, it is fully refundable after a certain length of time, provided the consumer makes consecutive satisfactory payments. The deposit could take a few to several months to be received, depending upon the service provider's guidelines, and consumers may have to request the refund. Telecommunication, electric, natural gas, and water providers may use specially designed scoring models to assist them in making credit offers, as do other industries. Normally, if an applicant does not have prior experience paying for a utility or telecommunication service, instead of completely denying the service, a deposit will be required; however, there are instances when no deposit will be required nor will restrictions or special conditions apply to the service. Even services that have been established without deposits or limitations may be subject to adverse actions during the life cycle of the account. In the same manner as credit grantors, utility and telecommunication providers may periodically review consumers' accounts (particularly payment history) and take adverse action. The most common adverse action is to charge a deposit after the account has been established and experienced a series of delinquent payments. This deposit will be attached to a future billing statement and act as a resource to secure final payment after the service has been disconnected (by a consumer). If the final bill amount is less than the deposit assessed, the service provider will issue a refund for the difference. Conversely, if the final bill amount exceeds the deposit ascertained, the consumer will be billed for the remaining balance.

Noncompliance of federal requirements

Utility and telecommunication service providers must also adhere to federal laws prescribed by the Fair Credit Reporting Act. In September 2004, two of the nation's largest telecommunication providers (Sprint and AT&T) were charged with violating portions of the Fair Credit Reporting Act. The two companies, which placed restrictions on the services offered to some consumers (that is, deposits and spending limits) were accused of not advising consumers of their rights to receive free copies of their credit reports and dispute errors contained in them. Anytime limitations are placed on consumers' telephone services, the providers are required by federal law to completely notify them of certain rights. As a result of several consumer complaints and further investigation, the Federal Trade Commission requested that the United States Department of Justice file a formal complaint. Consequently, Sprint paid more than $1,000,000 and AT&T paid more than $350,000 in civil penalties. In addition, both companies agreed to standard record-keeping guidelines to aid the Federal Trade Commission in determining their future compliance to the Fair Credit Reporting Act.

Like other industries that establish business relationships with consumers, utility and telecommunication providers' practices are also monitored and regulated. Most, if not all states have public utility or public service commissions. These organizations are charged with regulating telecommunication, electric, natural gas, and water utilities, among other services. In addition to ensuring the safety of such services to consumers, they are active in making sure those services are offered at reasonable rates. Most importantly, public utility commissions may assist consumers in rectifying ongoing, unresolved complaints against various service providers. However, as a rule, they strongly recommend (or require) that consumers contact the service providers directly and attempt to resolve issues on their own first. If no progress is made, they suggest filing a complaint, detailing the nature of the dispute. These useful organizations may be instrumental in helping consumers who have attempted to correct an issue they have experienced with a utility or telecommunication service provider. They generally receive complaints from consumers regarding billing errors, disconnection of services, unauthorized account modifications and repair problems. Consumers may determine how to contact the public utility commission agency in their state of residence by searching the Internet or using a local telephone book. Complaints regarding rights as legislated under the Fair Credit Reporting Act may still be addressed to the Federal Trade Commission at *http://www.ftc.gov*.

Chapter summary

Credit plays a vital role in not only securing charge cards and various types of loans, but it has an integral part in helping to obtain other types of services as well. This fact alone is more evidence to support how important it is for consumers to manage their credit wisely. Products and tools offered by credit-reporting companies (excluding traditional credit reports) are widely used by utility service providers to assist in making safer and more accurate credit decisions. Without applying for service, whether or not consumers will eventually be allowed to know if they have a delinquent debt listed in an exchange remains to be seen. Assuming that consumer discussion and concern about this resource flourishes, it very promising that this idea will come into fruition. In the meantime, consumers should remain aware that management of past credit obligations may play a significant role in establishing various essential utility services.

Chapter 4—Quiz

1. Other than completely denying credit, what adverse actions may utility providers take?

2. Establishing utility service in the identity of a minor is acceptable in most states. (True/False)

3. What are two common complaints that public utility/service commissions receive from consumers?

4. What is an "exchange"?

Chapter 4—Quiz Answers

1. Other than denying credit, utility companies may place restrictions on services offered.

2. False.

3. Billing errors and repair complaints are two common complaints that public utility/service commissions receive from consumers.

4. An "exchange" is a database of unpaid utility accounts that is often managed or owned by credit-reporting agencies.

Credit-
Reporting Agencies

Understanding credit-reporting agencies

W hat is a credit-reporting agency? What does a credit-reporting agency do? The average consumer has some idea of what these companies do, but is not cognizant of all the roles of credit-reporting agencies. Credit-reporting agencies are subunits of larger corporations and are branded information service companies.

Equifax, Experian and Trans Union are all known as credit-reporting companies, but some clarification is necessary. All three are information services companies, meaning they practice the business of collecting, sharing and selling information, mainly information about consumers, though not exclusively. However, the credit-reporting segments of these corporations carry slight name variations from their company name. For example, Trans Union's consumer-reporting division is called Trans Union Consumer Relations, Equifax's is Equifax Consumer Services and Experian's is Experian National Consumer Assistance Center.

Often, consumers contact credit-reporting agencies with the assumption that they are debt collectors working on behalf of creditors. While some credit-reporting agencies may have risk management and debt recovery divisions, they do not exist primarily to act as collection companies. Other consumers contact credit-reporting agencies wishing for them to accept payment(s) on behalf of the creditors to whom money is owed. Credit-reporting agencies are not debt management companies, however, nor do they receive payments on behalf of creditors.

The aforementioned statements are just a few myths many consumers have and perpetuate about credit-reporting companies. These, and other misconceptions, often cause consumers to take a defensive, aggressive approach that is not necessary when contacting credit-reporting agencies. The rumors, half-truths and misinformation must be totally dispelled in order to create savvy, educated consumers.

The good old days

Prior to the establishment of credit-reporting agencies as they are known today, credit grantors used manual, time-consuming strategies to screen applicants and determine the best candidates for credit. Most of the grantors had entire departments in place that verified an applicant's repayment behavior with other creditors. Consumers would actually provide the names of their creditors as references on their credit applications. The references were then contacted to confirm the pay history of the applicant. Most of the verification was completed by telephone. As you can imagine, there were probably many messages left between the various parties involved in this tedious, painstaking process.

Another adverse side effect of this antiquated process was the length of time it took to make a final decision. With such a manually intensive process, receiving a quick yes or no answer was virtually impossible for consumers. As credit grantors began to grow, it became even more difficult and cumbersome to confirm an applicant's payment history and eligibility in order to make business decisions. Not only was this process time-consuming and inefficient, it was also very expensive because credit grantors had to hire, train and maintain a staff to meet these organizational needs.

Introducing credit-reporting agencies

Before long, some creditors thought it would save both time and money to have a central resource to store and maintain all consumer repayment information. Credit grantors would then be able to contact the managers of this central site and receive a summary of an applicant's repayment history. The third parties designated to manage the centralized repository of information would come to be known as credit-reporting agencies (or consumer-reporting agencies).

In order to supply a report summary that was most useful, various creditors had to agree to submit periodic updates to credit-reporting agencies regarding the repayment patterns of their customers. While much more ingenious than the previous method, this process was still far from perfect. Needless to say, it would take time, technology and a great deal of patience in order to transform this blueprint into a more useful resource and for it to operate with optimal efficiency.

Thanks to computers and legislation, over time, additional value was built into the new process. Eventually, automation would drive the credit verification process, bringing into existence credit scoring and substantial income potential for software developers such as Fair Isaac and Company. In addition, credit-reporting agencies would begin offering fraud alerts to aid in the prevention fraud. These enhancements increased the efficiency of the credit application process and aided in deterring unauthorized use of consumers' personal information.

In order for credit grantors to take advantage of the benefits offered by this new, creative process, they had to establish business relationships with credit-reporting companies. Obviously, this process allowed creditors to reduce the sizes of certain departments and make better use of their human resources. As a result of streamlining the credit-verification process, the roles, responsibilities and uses of credit-reporting agencies have significantly expanded. The credit-reporting agencies have shaped their businesses and markets to remain competitive and profitable. A quick visit to any one of the reporting agencies Websites will reveal an array of products and services available for consumers and business customers to purchase.

In addition to the agencies proactively recognizing buying patterns and creating wanted or needed services, many industries have sought them for assistance in determining various consumer trends. Buying habits often indicate the trends and desires of consumers, and many businesses realize the knack credit-reporting agencies have for collecting and maintaining this information.

Obviously, the information they store has huge income potential. For example, some credit-reporting agencies may have divisions that provide employment verification, background checks and even offer certain services to providers of insurance. Most recently, the United States government has solicited assistance from credit-reporting agencies in the war on terrorism. Credit-reporting agencies are able to provide financial data on consumers that is obtained directly from credit reports. The specifics surrounding credit-reporting agencies' roles in helping to fight the war on terror will be discussed in more detail in an upcoming chapter, but these are a few ways in which the authority and uses of credit-reporting companies have been heightened since their creation.

What credit-reporting agencies do

Credit-reporting agencies exist primarily to store and maintain data on consumers' debt repayment patterns. Credit-reporting agencies begin recording repayment information shortly after a consumer establishes an account with a creditor (usually between 30 and 90 days following the initiation of an agreement). Creditors have relationships with reporting agencies that allow them to submit periodic updates (monthly or bimonthly) on consumers' repayment behaviors. In terms of consumer-initiated accounts, credit-reporting agencies do not go to creditors soliciting information about repayment patterns. Instead, consumers' creditors willingly supply this information to them. In this light, credit-reporting agencies are not the underhanded snoops that they are frequently accused of being. They actually have business relationships with creditors allowing them to report consumer credit behavior. Other consumer debts such as liens, garnishments, bankruptcies and judgments are obtained in a different fashion. Credit-reporting companies often have established partnerships with vendors who frequent county, state and federal courts to retrieve such data from them. This data is then attached to consumers' credit records. In this aspect, reporting agencies may be living up to their infamous reputations of being snoops, because they are more proactive in gathering public record data. By allowing credit-reporting agencies to store and compile repayment patterns of consumers, the hundreds and thousands of creditors are able to make informed decisions to grant or deny credit with minimal research. It's a safe, cost-effective and fast method of making sound business decisions.

Consumers should understand that credit-reporting agencies do not make decisions to grant or deny credit to consumers. This is the sole responsibility of creditors. The only role agencies play in the process is allowing creditors access to consumers' credit histories and reporting the information as provided to them. The idea that credit reporting agencies grant and deny credit is by far the grandest fallacy consumers tend to have. Credit-reporting agencies do not even make recommendations to creditors about which applications to accept or reject; they are really a neutral, unbiased party in the credit application process.

Credit-reporting companies are also charged with the onerous task of helping consumers maintain accurate information in their credit records and providing complete disclosure of their credit records upon request. Consumers cannot be denied their right to know the content of their credit reports as long as they properly identify themselves. Identifying oneself may consist of revealing personal information such as Social Security numbers, complete legal names, addresses and dates of birth. Consumers failing to properly identify themselves to credit-reporting companies may encounter challenges that will make the disclosure process a difficult and time-consuming one. Properly identifying oneself helps to protect the confidentiality of a consumer's personal credit information and helps the reporting agency locate the appropriate credit records.

Credit-reporting agencies store millions upon millions of credit records in their databases. When consumers contact a credit-reporting agency to request verification of suspicious or erroneous information appearing in their credit records, the credit-reporting agency has five business days upon receipt of the request to begin its formal investigation. The investigation consists of a reporting agency contacting the source(s) of the disputed information and verifying its accuracy.

The credit-reporting agency must also review and consider any relevant documentation provided to it by a consumer. Relevant documents include any legitimate material that supports a consumer's claim that an item is reflecting incorrect information. Some examples include statements and various letters from creditors, identification documents (a driver's license, Social Security card or birth certificate), credit bureau correction letters and police reports. The credit-reporting agency must notify the creditors identified as reporting erroneous information of all relevant documents received from a consumer supporting his or her claim.

A credit-reporting company then has 30 calendar days (21 for residents of Maine) to conduct and complete its investigation of the items contested by a consumer. Upon completion of an investigation, a credit-reporting agency must notify a consumer (in writing) of the results of the investigation, supply a revised credit report and provide contact information of creditors supplying the information in question. In some states (California, Colorado, Maryland, New Jersey and New York), the credit-reporting agencies must send revised credit reports to all creditors the consumer has applied to for credit within the past six or 12 months (depending on location), if the consumer makes this request.

Not all credit grantors report accounts to credit-reporting agencies. Companies that generally report are big names that are regionally or nationally recognized. A few examples of nationally recognized companies that report are Bank of America, Citibank, Capital One and First Consumers National Bank. Regional creditors are sometimes more popular in certain geographical areas of the country. Some examples include Branch Bank & Trust (southeastern United States), various credit unions, Belk department store and Bank of America (northeastern United States).

Often, consumers who do business with smaller, unfamiliar banks run the risk of not having a credit report that reflects all of their past accounts. Small creditors do not generally report to credit-reporting agencies. Instead, consumers should determine if the creditor reports to the major agencies before opening an account.

Companies that have business relationships with credit-reporting agencies pay for use of its services; they are not able to access consumer credit files or report account repayment information freely. Perhaps this is the reason why smaller credit grantors often do not report. If a creditor does not have a business relationship with a credit-reporting agency, it cannot report consumer account activity.

Additionally, there are some creditors who only submit information to reporting agencies when a consumer's account defaults. Utility companies who supply gas and electricity, as well as apartment leasing offices, are known to partake in this practice. Hence, a consumer may be denied a service such as telephone or electricity for this reason.

It is always a good idea to find out whether a potential creditor reports to a credit-reporting agency, especially if a consumer is trying to establish credit. While most major credit grantors report to all three national credit-reporting agencies, there are some who only have business relationships with a select one. Ask to find out specifics prior to establishing an account with a potential creditor. Creditors are not required by law to report consumer repayment history to credit-reporting agencies. However, if they choose to do so, they are equally responsible for helping consumers maintain accurate information in their credit records.

Fraud

Credit-reporting agencies also assist consumers in helping to protect their credit and personal identification from being used without their consent. Most reporting agencies offer fraud alerts that aid in the prevention of a culprit establishing unauthorized credit using a consumer's identity. This is sometimes referred to as a "hawk alert." The alert asks that a consumer be contacted in writing or via telephone prior to any offer of credit being extended in his or her name. It is merely a statement attached to a consumer's credit record that flags the attention of any creditor that accesses the file. These flags may be added free of charge, per a consumer's request, and may remain for short periods (90 days) or extended lengths (seven years), depending upon whether true fraud has occurred or this has been requested as a preventative measure.

Consumers might encounter tradeoffs as a result of adding security alerts to their credit records. They may be required to provide identification documents to creditors inperson when applying for credit. Similarly, some consumers may not be able to subscribe to certain online services, such as the option to view and dispute their credit reports via the Internet or receive their credit scores online. These are relatively minute consequences when one considers the benefits of keeping access to his or her personal information limited to only those who have been authorized. In addition, the major agencies are working constantly to abate the certain limitations a fraud alert may cause.

For a fee, some credit-reporting agencies offer other services to aid in the prevention of fraud. One such service sends e-mail notifications to consumers each time a creditor inquiry is made and also allows consumers to receive frequent disclosure of their credit reports.

Consumers must be proactive in decreasing their chances of becoming victims of fraud. Once again, consumers should stay informed. Do so by ordering a credit report at least twice a year. Upon receipt of the report, review it carefully and highlight any items that may appear to be suspicious. Then contact the credit-reporting agency (or agencies) to obtain an address and/or telephone number of the company supplying any questionable data. Additionally, monthly credit card statements should be perused to determine if any unauthorized charges have been applied to the account. If so, notify the credit card company immediately. In the event that a statement is late, contact the creditor as soon as possible!

Also, exercise extreme caution when making online purchases or providing personal identification over telephone lines to an unsolicited caller. Keep documents containing account numbers and personal identification secure and never leave these types of documents lying around on a desk at work or in plain view at home. Material containing personal information that is not being stored for future use or reference should be discarded immediately. Purchasing an inexpensive paper shredder will assist in destroying these types of documents. Preapproved credit card applications, statement summaries (from banks, credit cards, mobile phones, retail stores, gas cards, loans and utilities) should all take a final visit to the shredder after they have been reviewed.

Other measures that some credit-reporting agencies take to help consumers in the prevention of fraud include blocking Social Security numbers from hard (paper) copies of credit reports sent via mail. In addition, they will sometimes block the last few digits of credit account numbers. As an additional measure, creditors will often mask or transpose portions of account numbers when submitting them to databases of credit-reporting companies. Credit-reporting agencies will continue to play a vital role in assisting consumers and the business community in the effort to limit unauthorized use of another's identity. Whether their involvement is proactive or sanctioned by our government, their positions in the credit-reporting process demands their presence and contributions.

What else do credit-reporting agencies do?

Until recently, credit-reporting agencies have struggled to make noticeable profits directly from consumers. The cost they sometimes assess for issuing a credit report is so sporadic and low that it probably only covers the actual cost it takes to hire employees or maintain a system to process the request. Now that federal law is requiring credit-reporting agencies to provide one free credit report to all consumers (regardless of the state of residence), the agencies may explore other opportunities fueled by consumer interest in order to offset their losses. Other than selling lists of consumer names and addresses for direct marketing or preapproved lists, credit-reporting agencies have always wondered how to cleverly tap into the huge, lucrative consumer market without the support of its customers.

Enter the world of direct-to-consumer products. Internet use has become the fast, convenient way of doing business and obtaining information for consumers. Credit-reporting agencies have taken advantage of this resource by making available to consumers an array of products and services via the World Wide Web. Such things as credit-scoring and credit-monitoring products fall under this heading. Many of these offerings were created in response to consumers demand to learn more about the intricacies of credit-reporting (for example, how a credit score is created), their desire to keep informed about changes on their credit files and, lastly, to head off any attempts made to use their credit or identities without authorization. These products and services are what are referred to as direct-to-consumer commodities.

Though Equifax was the first known credit-reporting agency to launch direct-to-consumer services, the other two national agencies have followed suit. This business is also very profitable. In 2002, Equifax had nearly five million consumers signed to its direct-to-consumer services, helping to generate 39 million dollars in revenue. More noteworthy, however, is the fact that the business grew by 91 percent in one year and consumer renewal rates are nearly 50 percent. Using this data to extrapolate future performance of direct-to-consumer business, it appears this sector will continue to be widely successful, reaping huge earnings for credit-reporting agencies.

Prior to the inception of direct-to-consumer products, many executives considered consumer assistance centers (at the reporting agencies) as being mostly nonprofit units. In fact, they were regarded as liabilities that were in place primarily because of legal mandates imposed by the federal government. This type of thinking has encouraged the corporations to separate their consumer response businesses from their direct-to-consumer businesses, sometimes making them function as two independent divisions within the same company. Though most of the initial piloting to determine consumer demand for certain products is performed through the consumer service centers, the finished products are usually launched and serviced elsewhere.

One major credit-reporting agency, Equifax, offers consumers a home valuation product. This is a service that helps consumers make more informed decisions during the home-buying or home-selling process. For a fee of $5.95, consumers may receive property records of one home. In addition, this service provides sales figures of other homes in the same neighborhood that have recently been purchased or sold. For a fee of $19.95, a consumer may receive property and sales information of five different homes. Considering the current home-buying frenzy across the United States, Equifax has seized a valuable opportunity and created a very useful and timely product for consumers. At the time of this writing, it is the only credit-reporting agency I know of that is offering such a service. To learn more about this product, please visit *www.econsumer.equifax.com*.

Credit-reporting agencies also offer a wide array of products to their business customers. It's only fair that we consider these offerings as well. For starters, credit-reporting agencies offer products to aid creditors, particularly those making collection efforts, in recovering bad debts or delinquent accounts. Most, if not all, of the reporting companies can provide what's known in the industry as a collection report to some of its customers.

Have you ever attempted to dodge a creditor by moving or changing your contact numbers and conveniently forgetting to inform the debtor of your new contact information? Things are smooth for a while, right. You think: "I'm so sick of those letters and phone calls, I'm glad I ditched them." Then all of a sudden, the creditor embarrasses you by calling your place of employment or sends you another threatening letter! I'm here to tell you that your debtor may have been able to locate you thanks to a collection report provided by Experian, Equifax or Trans Union. The collection report is a summary of two of the most important factors collectors use to identify which debtors appear to have the best recovery potential, credit information and contact information.

Some of the information collection reports contain include notification that a consumer has recently filed for bankruptcy, names and addresses of other creditors (a collector may contact your other creditors to determine the most recent contact information you provided to them), notification that recent credit accounts have been opened, available credit limits of revolving accounts (this is why your collectors may often say to you: "Why don't you just make the payment using your credit card") and the name and address of a consumer's employer (this is how collectors call you at work).

To clarify, the collection report may not give the account numbers of a consumer's credit cards, but it does reveal whether there is existing credit available. In addition, collectors may have to do additional research to obtain the telephone number or address of a consumer's employer, as most credit-reporting agencies have outdated employment information (and even those who do have current information do not often have the addresses and phone numbers).

Credit-reporting agencies may also provide products (collection models) that help debt recovery companies determine which delinquent accounts are most collectible and also help them prioritize their collection efforts. I'm almost positive that most consumers are not aware of this information. This supports my theory of how all sectors of the credit-reporting industry work together to maintain a circulatory process. How many consumers knew that creditors help other creditors determine your whereabouts?

Other services credit-reporting agencies offer its business customers iclude:

- Portfolio management tools—they help businesses evaluate accounts to separate the most profitable ones from the least profitable, they help identify other money-making opportunities with existing customer base by identifying trends, they provide risk-reduction techniques and they help evaluate existing business practices to improve them.

- Direct-marketing tools—consumer e-mail or address lists to make preapproved offers. These lists may also be classified to help businesses cater their offers (prime versus sub-prime).

- Bankruptcy notification tools—agencies identify recent consumer bankruptcy filings.

- Compliance tools (Fair Credit Reporting Act including Fair and Accurate Transactions Act).

- Fraud tools—authentication tools, fraud prediction tools and identifying high-risk applicants.

- Small business credit reports—offered by Equifax. It is the first credit-reporting agency to offer such reports and compete with Dun & Bradstreet, the leading information services company that provides data on the credit standings of businesses.

Chapter summary

As the needs of consumers and credit grantors have changed, our credit-reporting system has gracefully evolved. Interrelated processes have a tendency to influence growth and change in each other. Credit-reporting agencies are linked to larger information service corporations and have aided in alleviating many of the initial burdens that are byproducts of manual processes. Their contributions have significantly abated the time needed to make an intelligent, informed decision about an applicant's creditworthiness. Both credit grantors and consumers can appreciate the proficiency of the credit verification process today as opposed to the antiquated one used several years ago. While this has been the primary function of credit-reporting agencies, we see that their boundaries and uses have been extended much further and will continue to be stretched in order to maximize their usefulness and marketability for consumers. How well do you understand the core functions of credit-reporting agencies? Take the following quiz to find out.

Chapter 5—Quiz

1. Credit-reporting agencies accept and reject applications for credit. (True/False)

2. Do credit-reporting agencies collect payments for outstanding debts?

3. How do credit-reporting agencies obtain public record information on consumers?

4. How many days does a credit-reporting agency have to begin a reinvestigation once notified of an error from a consumer?

5. All creditors report to at least one national credit-reporting agency. (True/False)

*** Bonus: Who supplies credit-reporting agencies with most of their information?

Chapter 5—Quiz Answers

1. False

2. Credit-reporting agencies do not collect payments for outstanding debts.

3. Credit-reporting agencies obtain public record information about consumers by third-party vendors.

4. Once notified of an error, a credit-reporting agency has five business days to begin a formal investigation.

5. False

*** Bonus: Furnishers and creditors supply credit-reporting agencies with most of their information.

Credit Scoring

What's the score?

Credit scoring is an aspect of consumer credit that has experienced a noteworthy amount of growth and popularity. Today, consumers are more concerned about their credit scores than almost any other facet of credit. Credit-reporting agencies, financial advisors and resellers alike have also taken advantage of consumer interest in the credit-scoring market by offering services that provide individual scores. Some of the products available will even allow consumers to manipulate credit data and predict how the changes will affect their scores. Others simply provide consumers advice on how to improve their credit ratings and scores. Creditors have begun increasing their use of scores to assist in the application process. In fact, it is more common for merchants to make credit decisions exclusively based on a consumer's credit score than ever before. Why is there such a big frenzy about credit scoring, and why are many people consumed with it? Everything you need to know about credit scoring will be discussed in this chapter.

Credit scoring allows creditors to make quick decisions regarding the extension of credit. Upon accessing a consumer's credit record in a credit-reporting agency's database, credit grantors receive a number (credit score) along with a list of debts a consumer is responsible for repaying. Frankly, a credit score is a number that determines risk. It predicts how likely a consumer is to either default or pay on time based upon how that consumer is currently handling credit, how he or she has handled credit in the past and his or her current level of debt. In essence, it is triggered by all existing account information appearing on a consumer's credit report. Therefore, it is imperative that the content of a consumer's credit record is accurate. Incomplete, erroneous data on a credit record will lead to a distorted credit score and possibly the denial of credit. To what extent the score will be distorted depends on how pervasive the errors are.

Why credit scores are important

There are some creditors who regard credit scores (exclusively) as gospel. Regardless of any extenuating circumstances, many of them will live and die (so to speak) by their predetermined criteria and score cutoffs (minimum score accepted to offer a consumer credit).

Other creditors may be a bit more flexible when making credit decisions. They will usually try to work with consumers that may not have met cutoffs but scored close, or entertain extending credit to consumers that have very little or no existing credit by closely considering outside elements such as income and employment history.

The truth is credit grantors do not have to rely solely on credit scores to make decisions; they are not required to do so. They may override score cutoffs if they choose to. If this action is taken, it is probably going to be determined after other important factors not derived from a credit report are considered. For the most part, scores are very reliable predictors of future credit performance; this is why many credit grantors and lenders depend so heavily on them. Credit scores not only allow grantors to determine if they should offer consumers credit, they also help in determining what type of rates are available to a given consumer. This magical number, regardless of other elements, may be the driving factor in determining whether a consumer gets the titanium, platinum, gold or standard credit card.

Software models score credit records systematically. Companies such as Fair Isaac and Company create the scoring software algorithms. Credit-scoring companies such as Fair Isaac and Company partner with credit-reporting agencies to develop systems that evaluate the previous credit performance of a sample of consumers. The repayment behavior of the sample is considered over a certain length of time; three years for example. The various patterns are studied to determine which factors indicate how likely a consumer may be to repay a debt on time or default. These evaluations consider various types of credit, such as loans and charge cards. Those categories may be further subdivided into categories such as mortgages and automobile and personal loans, or major credit cards and retail department store cards.

Many consumers mistakenly believe that credit-reporting agencies score credit records and then suggest to creditors names of consumers who should be extended credit and names of those who should not. This is a common fallacy. Credit-reporting agencies assist mostly in the developmental process of creating scoring models. More specifically, they provide input on categories and traits that they want to have the scoring model consider when evaluating a credit record.

Since credit-reporting agencies get most of their business from credit grantors, they routinely receive requests from their customers on how to identify the best candidates to offer credit to (the best meaning those with the lowest risk). Creditors help by providing the sample groups to be studied for common characteristics or behavior. For example, credit-reporting agencies may have many customers who are interested in limiting the amount of capital they lose due to consumers filing bankruptcy on their debts. After carefully analyzing a sample of consumers who have filed for bankruptcy, characteristics from their credit histories are identified and serve as indicators of other consumers who may file for bankruptcy in the future. The most frequent traits identified are recorded, along with any other significant predictive characteristics, and then provided to companies that design scoring software.

Credit-reporting agencies may specify which traits they want the model to evaluate and prioritize the categories representing those traits. Each category may contain several characteristics. The model will assign a point value to each trait observed and tally up the total amount of points earned in each category. The numbers earned in each category will be added together to create a final number. This number results in a credit score. (See the sample scorecard on following page for a detailed example. The sample scorecard and traits shown are not indicative of how all scoring models work and should not be used to predict how your credit will be evaluated with any creditor. Please note that it is only intended to be used as a guide in helping you to understand how credit scoring works in a general sense.)

After a scoring model is created, it will be packaged with a name (for example, Equifax's is referred to as Beacon, Experian's is known as the Experian/Fair Isaac Risk Model and Trans Union goes by the name of Empirica) and marketed to creditors as a tool designed to predict credit risk by objectively evaluating a credit record. In the following example, the model was designed to predict how likely it was that certain consumers would file bankruptcy. The three scoring models mentioned are above the most popular among lenders of credit, but there are enhanced models and custom models designed to evaluate other types of credit risks. Lenders, however, may use factors outside of those in a credit score or report help make a more informed and sound decision to extend or deny credit.

Different scoring models are created for different purposes. For example, one model may be used to help determine which consumer behavior is most likely to result in the default or foreclosure of a home loan; another may be designed to predict what consumer credit patterns indicate that a credit card may be charged off within a few years; still another may be created to evaluate which consumer traits often result in default of utility accounts. Credit scoring is a very intricate process, but due to its explosive popularity and widespread use among creditors, consumers have demanded more information about how it works. Residents of California may even receive their credit scores when they order a copy of their credit reports. Further, if they have applied for credit and been denied, the score may be sent free of charge! This is the type of consumer demand that keeps the public educated and apprised of existing and new credit processes.

Scorecard for Jane Consumer				
Category 1 (35%)	Trait One	Trait Two	Trait Three	Score
Timeliness of payments	Number of public record filings	Number of items in collections	Number of recent delin-quenies on accounts	
Possible Points	100	100	115	315
Points Earned	**52**	**73**	**48**	**173**
Category 2 (30%)	Trait One	Trait Two	Trait Three	Score
Level of debt	Balance to credit limit ratio on re-volving accounts	Amount owed on installment loans	Unpaid collection balances	
Possible Points	100	100	70	270
Points Earned	**43**	**44**	**70**	**157**
Category 3 (15%)	Trait One	Trait Two	Trait Three	Score
Length and age of credit	Age of credit history	Average age of revolving accounts	Average age of installment accounts	
Possible Points	40	40	55	135
Points Earned	**27**	**37**	**51**	**115**

(Chart continued on next page.)

Category 4 (10%)	Trait one	Trait two	Trait three	Score
New Credit Being Sought	Number of personal loan in-queries within past 60 days	Number of credit card inqueries within past 60 days	Number of retailer inquiries in past 60 days	
Possible Points	30	30	30	90
Points Earned	**30**	**30**	**30**	**90**
Category 5 (10%)	Trait One	Trait Two	Trait Three	Score
Type of credit	Number of re-volving accounts	Number of Installment accounts	Number of open accounts	
Possible Points	35	35	20	90
Points Earned	**30**	**31**	**20**	**81**
Total Possible				900
Final Credit Score				**616**

Reason Codes: Number of installment accounts established.
Number of recent delinquencies on revolving accounts.
Number of unpaid collection balances.
Age of revolving accounts too new.

What factors does a scoring model consider?

First, know that credit scores change as often as credit entries change. For example, if a credit record has received two brand new account balances, that indicates more debt; if one credit card is paid thirty days late, that indicates a recent delinquency that may not have appeared one month earlier; if a negative account purges from a credit record, that signifies one fewer negative entry. It follows that credit scores will change as consumers maintain their debts on a monthly basis. Taking a closer look at score models, let's discuss the specific areas they evaluate.

The basic models (Beacon, Experian and Emperica) consider de-linquencies, overall amount of debt, the length of time credit has been established, the frequency of inquiries (number of new credit accounts being sought) and type of credit already established. Some factors excluded by scoring models include age, race, gender, address, employment status and income. For companies that make decisions based entirely on a score, consider the following hypothetical situation. A consumer who has a six-figure income is denied a $500 retail card. If this lender makes credit decisions based solely on a credit score, the six-figure income is not a factor and is not observed by the scoring model.

The basic scoring models prioritize the aforementioned categories with respect to the general population as follows:

- Current and previous credit performance. This includes the number of months since the most recent delinquency, the frequency of slow pays, the most severe delinquency and the total number of delinquencies. The delinquencies refer to late payments on accounts, reports of collection agency debts and public record entries on a credit record. While some creditors may keep internal records of all late payments, they only report delinquencies of 30 days or more to credit-reporting agencies.

- Amount of debt. This includes balances on revolving and installment accounts, balance to credit limit ratio on revolving accounts and the balance to original amount ratio of installment accounts.

- Length of time credit has been established. This refers to the age of a credit record, considering the age of the oldest account and the median age of all established accounts.

- Inquiries. The inquiries are evaluated to determine how often a consumer is applying for credit. The only types of inquires observed are those that are initiated by a consumer for credit purposes. These types of inquiries are commonly labeled "hard inquiries." Promotional inquiries, employment inquiries and those performed by an existing creditor for review or monitoring purposes are bypassed by scoring models. Conversely, these types of inquiries are commonly referred to as "soft inquiries." Certain types of purchases often warrant price shopping for the most competitive bargain. Unfortunately, this could result in the accumulation of several inquiries in a very short period of time. Home and automobile buying are two prime examples. To avoid punishing consumers for price shopping, general scoring models will combine auto and mortgage inquiries into a single inquiry if they have occurred within the same 14-day period. Other consumer-initiated credit inquiries occurring within the past 12 months may be observed, but will have minimal impact on a credit score, as this entire category is very low in priority for factors considered by basic scoring models. Often, mortgage loan officers and auto sales personnel overkill the weight inquiries have in the scoring process. They look at their customers' credit records and if there is no conspicuous sign of slow pays, they assume the "X" factor must be the inquiries. Some of these sales people will even assign a random point value to each inquiry, say two points each, and filter this erroneous information to the buying public.

♦ Types of credit established. Most scoring models will look for a mixture of various types of credit (revolving, installment and open). Use of various types of credit may indicate a consumer's ability to manage different types of debts wisely. This category is also low in priority in terms of the weight it carries in affecting a credit score.

The categories that have the most substantial impact on scoring are the amount of current debt and previous/current credit performance. Scores for general models range from about 300–900. Typically, the higher the score, the lower the risk and the more likely a consumer will be to get approved on a credit application. Presently, the average consumer credit score in the United States falls near 700. This does not mean a consumer with a lower score will be denied credit, it merely indicates an average. Remember cutoffs and score standards are determined by individual lenders and may vary from lender to lender. In each of the aforementioned categories, there is a maximum of points that can be earned. The scoring model automatically deducts points for each trait (in a given category) that has an adverse factor or each category that lacks a characteristic that it has been designed to evaluate. All points earned in each category are added together to create the overall credit score.

When the score is generated, it will be accompanied by a list of the top four reason-codes that had the most impact on the resulting score. Reason-codes are determined by the largest variation between the highest amount of points possible and the actual amount of points earned in each observed category. These codes will vary depending on the content, repayment pattern and credit behavior identified on credit records being analyzed. Even credit records with the most kempt histories will return reason-codes. The reason-codes for credit records that have been meticulously maintained may seem inappropriate. For example, a reason code of "excessive inquiries" may be received for a credit record that shows two consumer-initiated inquiries within the past 12 months. If this consumer's credit record has no factors in the major categories that indicate poor credit performance or excessive outstanding debt, the model is going to move down the line and detect the next factor in order of priority that impacted the score. Most likely, this factor would not result in a denial of credit for a consumer with a healthy credit record, but would be identified as a reason for the score not being higher (because no other major factors triggered a greater variation between the amount of points possible and those actually earned).

A score could also return a reason-code citing "high balances..." when a credit record only has one or two accounts reflecting a balance. Unfortunately, most models do not have the ability to employ common sense or logic. They have been programmed with precise guidelines that they adhere to without any deviations whatsoever. For this reason, grantors should still carefully review credit applications before making final decisions to extend or deny credit. The human intellect is capable of applying impartial judgment and analysis of factors that a program-based software cannot. The previous is an example of an opportunity for lenders to override predetermined criteria and score cutoffs traditionally used. The model may generate such a reason-code because the one or two balances detected may be high with respect to their credit limits or original amount of the debt, as opposed to being generated because there is a substantial amount of outstanding debt on several accounts.

Additional information about credit scoring

Scoring models mathematically analyze various segments of a credit report to determine risk. The most popular scoring models employ the theory of "the higher the score, the lower the risk," but some models work in the exact opposite manner. These models employ the concept that a lower score equates to low risk, and a higher score to a high risk. These types of scoring models are mostly used in specialized fields of the credit and financial services industry and not for general lending purposes. General scoring models compare one consumer's credit use and repayment behavior to several other consumers' past credit performances. The current and past credit behavior is evaluated so that prior credit problems do not outweigh current accounts that are being managed responsibly. In fact, as adverse occurrences age, their impact in lowering a score decreases.

It's important to keep in mind that credit scores are generated individually rather than jointly. It follows that couples or multiple consumers applying for credit as a group will also receive individual scores. The scores are not averaged or combined; not even for married couples. There are also some credit entries that are not considered by the score. These include child support payment obligations and rental history items.

Some consumers are paranoid about their credit scores and the factors they believe will lower them. When contacting credit grantors and service providers to inquire about offers, these curious folks often are already aware of their scores and practically demand information from creditors. Upon contacting the lender, most likely the consumer will provide their score, which they received from one of the credit-reporting agencies or another source, and ask whether or not a deposit is required from them or what type of rates are available. This type of request is flawed and consumers should not waste their time asking for it.

The primary reason consumers do this is to avoid having another inquiry appear on their credit reports. Most have been conditioned to fear and avoid accumulation of inquiries by misinformed employees in various sectors of the financial services industry.

Furthermore, they are mistakenly convinced that the score received from one of the credit-reporting agency's products is their only score, when it is not. Depending upon the type of credit a consumer is inquiring about, the creditor or service provider may use a completely different scoring model from the generic one marketed to consumers by the credit-reporting agencies. In addition, the lender may use a custom model that considers other factors not derived from credit reports. For this reason, they perform their own credit checks before making credit offers to consumers. While it behooves consumers to ask about credit requirements when approaching a lender, they must understand that creditors will not rely on their words as evidence of how high their credit scores are.

Improving a credit score

Now that consumers have access to a plethora of information about credit scoring, they have an unquenchable desire to understand its vast, complex composition. The most fascinating aspect of scoring that consumers are determined to master is what they can do to improve or drive their scores up. Unfortunately, trial and error attempts to quickly alter account information with the hope of raising a score have only furthered consumer frustration.

At the behest of many uninformed financial services employees, consumers often contact creditors and make a myriad of changes to their accounts. The changes include, but are not limited to, closing revolving accounts, paying off balances on charged off installment accounts or collection agency items and public records. The truth is, there is no magical formula in existence to immediately raise a credit score other than paying off a substantial amount of debt on both revolving and installment accounts that are not old and delinquent.

Sometimes taking the advice of a loan officer to close revolving accounts may have an adverse impact and actually lower a score.

Remember, the basic models evaluate credit records for a good mixture of revolving and installment accounts. If all revolving lines of credit are closed, no use of revolving credit will be detected and could result in lowering a score. Financial services employees have a reputation of making suggestions to consumers that they think should raise their scores ("should" being the operative word). Consumers assume that these workers are skilled in their respective fields and acquiesce to the propositions being made. The loan officers, mortgage brokers and auto salespeople all have the same incentive. If you buy, they get paid. Therefore, it is only logical for them to perform and act with tenacity when a customer is bringing business to them. Believe it or not, these employees are not all selfish and greedy. Sometimes their motivation is twofold. On the one hand, they may receive a nice chunk of the sale; on the other, a consumer may be pressuring them for a more competitive rate. If a more competitive rate is not offered, the consumer will take his or her money and business elsewhere. Thus, if a consumer's score falls below a lender's cutoff or is too low to qualify for a special rate, the salesperson is going to study the credit report, consider the reason-codes returned (hopefully) and offer guidance to the potential buyer on how he or she may improve the original score. In this context, the salesperson is attempting to please his or her customer as well as make a sale. Not all of these employees are the money-hungry predators they are often portrayed to be.

The solution

Because there is no guaranteed quick fix to increasing a credit score, consumers should begin with understanding that it will take time, patience and responsibility. Making all payments on or before due dates will prevent slow pays from being reported on your credit record. If you are unable to make a payment or realize that you have inadvertently missed one, contact your creditor(s) immediately! Sometimes creditors will change due dates for revolving account payments. Others will add an additional payment to the existing terms of installment accounts. For example, instead of having a loan paid off in April of 2008, the final payment may be adjusted to May 2008. These adjustments can be made without a creditor ever reporting a delinquency to the credit-reporting agencies. However, the amount of times this offset may be requested will probably be limited. Lenders use discretion in these cases. If a consumer has a history of not making timely payments, such options may not be available. Some creditors will offer insurance that will automatically pay the minimum amount due on revolving accounts should a consumer experience an unexpected job loss or similar financial setback. Normally, a creditor will attach the cost of the insurance as a monthly fee to the relevant credit card.

Avoid opening and applying for new accounts that are not needed. Many consumers convince themselves that they will only use a credit card for emergency purposes, but find themselves with revolving accounts that have high balances in a matter of months. By this time, the balance is probably subject to higher rates because the low, introductory rate has expired. Opening new accounts with lenders should be reserved for cases that warrant a need, not a want. Retail stores try to convince consumers to apply for credit so that they may receive an additional 10 percent off purchases. Receiving an additional 10 percent off is not worth an additional inquiry on your credit report. Traditionally, credit card offers from retail and department stores also carry painfully high rates, yet another reason for consumers to avoid them at all costs.

Earlier, I told you that some financial advisors recommend adding children as authorized users in an effort to help them establish credit. Some have blindly led consumers to believe this will also give the child the same credit score of the parent or guardian. Again this is false. Now that you understand the five categories scoring models evaluate, you also know why the child would not have an identical credit score as the parent. The child is only going to have one account on his or her credit record (the one his parent listed him as an authorized user on) versus the parent that probably has several accounts established over a number of years. This factor alone means the mixture of credit, age of credit history and other factors are going to be different for the parent than the child. Therefore, they will not have identical credit scores.

Also, some advisors lead consumers to believe that closing a revolving account wipes out your credit history related to that account, which has a negative impact to your credit scores. This is also absolutely false. First of all, canceling an account does not remove the account from your credit report. If the account is fully paid and closed in good standing, it will remain on your credit report for up to 10 years from the date of last activity. If the account is closed and you're still making payments, the date of last activity will begin on the date you pay the account off. Closing the account does not wipe away your credit history; this is simply not true. Closing the account only affects your balance to available credit ratio, which is a component observed by scoring models.

What *not* to do to improve a credit score

Here are some things to avoid if you want to improve your overall credit score:

- Close open revolving accounts.
- Open or apply for new accounts for no valid reason.
- Avoid making payments on time or ignore late notices.
- Card hop (frequently open new accounts to transfer high-interest balances to those with lower rates).

What to do to improve a score or keep a good score

Time is a very important element in maintaining or improving your credit score. Follow the fundamental steps outlined below and you will be on the path to a better credit score and creditworthiness.

- Use existing credit wisely. Do not treat credit cards as money reserves of any sort. The basic rule is never purchase on credit if there are no funds in your checking or savings account to cover the expense at the time it is incurred.
- Keep balances on revolving accounts below 50 percent of the actual credit limit. For example, a credit card with

a $5,000 credit limit should not exceed a balance higher than $2,500.

+ If applying for credit and one of the reason-codes indicated refers to "high balances or level of debt," paying down (or paying off) current accounts will help increase your score.

+ Paying off older accounts that show delinquencies (for example, collections, chargeoffs, etc.) may not do much to increase your score because of the age of those items.

+ Finally, review your credit reports from the three national agencies at least once a year and 60 days prior to making any major purchases on credit. Doing so will help eliminate an inaccurate, lower score due to errors found on your credit report. Checking your credit record well in advance of significant purchases makes the application process much smoother. Most errors on credit reports are negative, such as late payments or even delinquent accounts that are not yours. These are definitely factors observed by Fair Isaac and Company's scoring models, and are very likely to lower a credit score.

What's new with credit scoring?

One credit-reporting agency, Experian, has taken a clear lead in enhancing the credit-scoring business. In fact, they have dedicated an entire unit of its corporation to developing more useful products for financial institutions. Experian-Scorex, based in Atlanta, Georgia (along with rivalry Equifax), has launched a refined scoring model with key benefits to financial companies wishing to make better credit decisions.

Scorex PLUS sets itself apart from traditional bureau scoring models and even custom bureau models. For starters, this innovative product combines two risk assessment categories into one complete package: one to evaluate risk for new accounts (acquisitions) and another to evaluate risk for existing accounts (retention). The traditional bureau models have been charged with being biased toward the existing account channel. In other words, critics say they are better at determining risks associated with credit decisions pertaining to established accounts as opposed to those related to new accounts. As a result, lenders have been forced to purchase custom bureau models to better evaluate risks associated with new accounts, and this can be very expensive.

Scorex PLUS allows lenders the option of manipulating the product, or interchanging assessment needs, to review risks of acquiring new or existing accounts all in one package. This makes business transactions more streamlined and brings an added element of convenience to lenders' processes. Another benefit of Experian's new product is that it works around various credit-report elements that prevent traditional and custom models from returning a score automatically. For example, the credit file being evaluated must have at least one account with a date reported within six months from the current date (evaluation date); if not, the entire credit file is ineligible to be scored, which forces lenders to manually review a consumer's credit record. Keep in mind that businesses save a great deal of money thanks to the automation of processes; therefore, adding a manual process is counterproductive.

The enhancements offered by Scorex PLUS reduce the number of kick-outs requiring manual review by broadening the parameters of the accounts that can be scored. Further, Scorex PLUS models can be used to evaluate a consumer's credit file as it appears in the databases of Trans Union and Equifax, as well as those of Experian. This means that it can be applied to the needs of those lenders (particularly mortgage lenders) who review a consumer's combined credit history (also know as a tri-merge report) as reported by all three major reporting agencies, prior to making credit decisions. Much like the traditional models, Scorex PLUS returns the top four reason-codes affecting the credit score.

Preliminary research has revealed that Scorex PLUS outperforms the traditional models in accurately predicting risks by more than 90 percent. Experian has recognized the potential opportunity in the credit-scoring business, and is the first of the three major credit-reporting agencies to compete with Fair Isaac and Company by offering its independent scoring product. In a nutshell, for consumers this means a much smoother and more efficient application process, as well as a quicker "congratulations you've been approved" or "unfortunately, we cannot extend an offer to you at this time."

No credit, no score

For the longest time, consumers who did not have credit established struggled to convince lenders that they were creditworthy. Usually, this batch of consumers had no alternative other than to convince a friend or relative to co-sign for them or to list them as authorized users on existing credit card accounts. Another risky alternative for this group was obtaining a department store charge card, which typically has painfully high annual percentage rates.

In a short while, the rules of credit scoring may be changing to lessen the burdens of consumers who have thin credit files or those who do not have any credit. Fair Isaac and Company is reportedly creating a new product or enhancement that is specifically designed to tabulate scores for consumers that do not have credit. The technology evaluates how these consumers handle bank accounts and other financial obligations that do not usually appear on consumer credit reports. This supports my previous recommendation for consumers to open checking and/or savings accounts to help them establish credit. Doing so is a benefit. The goal of the product is to determine the best candidates (those with the least default risks) to offer loans. However, as scoring model updates and enhancements are costly to lenders, it may take quite some time for the new technology to infiltrate and for consumers to realize its impact.

Chapter summary

As lenders and various service providers continue to automate processes to stifle costs and increase efficiencies, they are certain to maximize the technology of credit scoring. As scores will continue to be driving factors in determining if an offer will be made and what type of offer will be made, consumers will continue to be concerned about them. In retrospect, I remember not long ago, credit-reporting agencies cringed at the thought of consumers asking about credit scoring. Credit-reporting agencies have transformed a difficult topic that they once shunned and diverted attention away from into lucrative subunits of their businesses. Now, consumers have access to a plethora of information pertaining to credit scoring that has been previously unavailable.

As more consumers demand and inquire about the dynamics of this amazing phenomenon, its popularity will magnify and many companies will seize the opportunity to increase their profits. Because credit scoring is still relatively new, it is both expected and natural for curiosity to trigger consumer interest. However, the most significant notion regarding credit scoring still lies in the content of credit files and the accuracy of the information contained therein.

Consumers must be careful not to become so overwhelmed by the specifics of credit scoring (and what they can do to boost their scores) that this fact is forgotten or trivialized. Some are so consumed by their "score" that they appear to have placed a value on it that is synonymous with their merit as a person. Do not allow a numeric figure assigned by a software company and credit-reporting agency to determine your self-worth. Doing so would be ridiculous. Thinking of a credit score as one's reputation is a more realistic approach; once a person's reputation is tarnished, it generally takes time, good deeds and consistency to rebuild it. Credit scoring is no different.

Chapter 6—Quiz

1. What is a credit score?

2. Each inquiry deducts three points from a score. (True/False)

3. Who creates credit-scoring software?

4. Name two elements that a basic scoring model considers.

5. What are reason-codes?

6. What is a good score?

7. What should consumers do to ensure their credit scores are accurate?

8. Closing open accounts guarantees a higher score. (True/False)

*** Bonus: List two tips to help improve a credit score.

Chapter 6—Quiz Answers

1. A credit score is a number that predicts future credit performance.

2. False

3. Fair Isaac and Company is the leading creator of credit-scoring software.

4. Two elements a scoring model considers are prior paying history (late payments) and current amount of debt.

5. Reason-codes are comments generated by scoring models that reveal why a score was lower than possible or why a person was denied credit.

6. The meaning of a good score may vary depending upon creditors' unique criteria. What is considered good to one may not be good to another.

7. Consumers should make sure there are no mistakes on their credit files to ensure their scores are accurate.

8. False

*** Bonus: Paying accounts on or before due dates and keeping balances low may help improve a credit score.

Bargaining With Your Creditors

Being proactive and bold

The consumer who is not afraid to ask for a better deal or concessions has a better chance of saving on interest rates, avoiding late fees, preventing derogatory comments from appearing on his or her credit report and saving money on outstanding debts. Many consumers get stuck in bad contracts for years because they are simply afraid to speak up and ask for better deals. It never hurts to ask. Iisn't that what our parents taught us? Negotiating with your creditors will often allow you to head off credit problems before they are severely in default and the negative marks appended to your credit report. It may also allow you to get better deals on credit cards, loans and so on. In addition, you will be in a better position to maintain strong relationships with creditors. This chapter will give you some helpful tips on how to bargain with your creditors to maintain good relationships, keep your credit record clean and help keep you financially afloat. We'll discuss negotiating from the beginning phases of establishing credit, maintaining good credit, updating credit reports and even dealing with collectors to resolve outstanding balances.

Bargaining during the application process

The key to bargaining with businesses in the credit/financial world is to be proactive and confident. When you are considering applying for a credit card, loan or other form of credit, the first thing you should do is investigate what companies are offering the most competitive deals. This can be done by simply calling or visiting the Websites of banks, credit card providers and so on. Let's consider a variety of different purchases that we rely on credit for.

Auto shopping

Unless you have money falling out the sides of your pockets, you're probably not going to visit your local Toyota dealer and pay for the Camry you want with cash. Many consumers visit auto dealers and allow them to finance their car, or select the bank that will handle the financing. Doing so does not always provide consumers with the best offers in terms of rates.

Once you know the price of the vehicle you want, do your own automobile loan shopping. This means you should contact banks and financing companies on your own and let them know you're inquiring about current loan rates. Let them know that you're purchasing a vehicle and advise them of the amount needed for the automobile. You can start by contacting the bank you already have a checking, savings or other account with. In many cases, your bank will appreciate your loyalty and reward you by offering a very competitive rate, especially if you have multiple accounts with it such as a mortgage, credit card, savings or checking. If another bank is offering a better rate for the same type of loan, challenge your bank to match it or take your business to the other one.

Employee credit unions are also great sources of finding competitive rates. If your employer has one, by all means join. When you call to inquire about rates, the banks can tell you the best rates they're offering without them having to pull your credit report. Therefore, if you contact one of them and its best rate is 11.9 percent, go on to the next bank and see what it is offering.

Additionally, do not allow any bank to check your credit report until you've decided that it is offering the best rate. Don't be fooled into thinking the bank has to run your credit to determine the best rates available. In reality, your credit is being checked to see if you can be approved for the best rate the bank is offering; and in some cases, the best rate a bank is offering is not what we consider competitive. Do you see the difference? The down payment that you would have normally given to the auto dealer can be applied to the loan you've found independently, thereby reducing the principal amount of it.

Once you have located the financial institution offering the best deal, then you can apply for the loan. If approved for the best rate, you can begin visiting automobile dealers to test-drive the vehicle you want. We are so accustomed to doing the opposite (visiting dealerships and test-driving first, and then obtaining financing). The bottom line is we have to change the way we shop. We'll get better deals that way. Trust me; it makes your car shopping experience almost completely hassle-free. When you visit the car lot and the dreaded question arises about your credit standing or credit score, you can simply reply: "I've already acquired my own financing." How liberating does that statement sound?

The only thing you'll have to do is negotiate the price of the vehicle you're purchasing, keeping in mind the amount of the loan you've already been approved for, including taxes. Because you've already obtained your own loan, the greatest part is you don't have to worry about have 10 auto-financing inquiries appended to your credit report. Even though they have minimal impact on your credit score, they're messy and you are certainly better off without them. You can also try this method with home loans, personal loans and insurance as well. Good luck!

Credit Cards

When considering applying for a credit card, follow the same advice I gave you for auto shopping. Contact various credit card companies and simply ask what rates are currently available. Some additional questions that come to mind are "Are there annual membership fees?" "Is this a fixed rate or is it variable?" "Is this just an introductory rate" "Should I experience financial hardships in the future, do you offer insurance that will make the minimum payment for me?" and "Do your contracts include universal default clauses?"

A universal default clause means that the credit card company can hike up your rates if it discovers by reviewing your credit record that you've defaulted on another debt obligation. For example, let's say you recently had a 30-day-late payment on your auto loan and this appears on your credit report. Although you've never missed a payment to your credit card company, this clause allows them to increase your current rate. Though most credit card companies exercise the universal default clause, you may be able to find a few that do not. Much like shopping for auto loans, your local bank or employee credit union is a great place to start when credit card shopping.

Bargaining after an account has been established

Obviously, if you are trying to establish credit for the first time or reestablish credit after experiencing a financial setback, your chances of getting the best rates are slim to impossible. However, you may be approved for a higher, sub-prime rate. In this case, you may have to temporarily accept the higher rate. Make sure your purchases are well within what you're capable of repaying in 30 days and, above all, make all of your payments on or before their due date. In addition, pay your other credit obligations on time.

After about six months of timely payments, call the credit card issuer and begin to negotiate. Using the past six months of excellent payment history as your premise, tell the credit card company that you deserve a more competitive rate and then ask for the current one to be lowered. The credit card company will probably ask you to hold as the agent reviews your payment history, credit report and so on. Hopefully, the representative will return with a lower offer. Again, if you are establishing or reestablishing credit, the rate may not be perfect, but it's better than what you previously had.

After another six months of positive repayment behavior, try again to get the rate reduced to an even lower one. By the end of the first year, you may be able to apply with another credit card company and get a better offer because you've paid everything on time for 12 consecutive months.

If you acquire a better rate from a new credit card company, you can call the one with the higher rate and ask it to match the offer. Point out your good payment history, including the fact that you've made payments before the due date and your customer loyalty. If the company refuses to match the better offer, call its bluff and suggesting closing the account. Normally, if you say the forbidden words, "I want to close this account," the credit card company will make concessions and give you the rate you're asking for, or at least try to.

Retail and department store cards will probably not budge on the rates being offered. For some unknown reason, these institutions traditionally have the highest rates among revolving accounts, even if the consumer is not a risky candidate. It's still worth a try to negotiate with them. The least they can say is "At this time, 24.9 percent is our best offer."

In the past couple examples, I've told you how to contact banks and creditors directly and how to be an initiator. Doing so is taking a proactive approach; this is an important step in taking control of your finances overall. If you're reactive versus proactive, you will frequently get stuck with bad deals. Remember that your creditors are in business to make money, not to make your life or standard of living lavish. If they're going to offer lower rates, they'd prefer doing business with someone that has low risk. Make sure that your repayment behavior is positive, meaning you've paid on time, and then be proactive. Be bold and ask for a better deal.

How to deal with being late

Even the most organized and detailed consumer sometimes misses a payment by its due date. Sometimes we know we're going to be late and sometimes we simply forget. Again I advise you to be proactive. If you're aware that your funds are short and you're just not going to be able to make the payment by the due date, contact your creditor immediately. If the creditor is a credit card company, it may record the payment late. But as a "one-time courtesy," they might waive the $29 late fee.

The beauty of the credit-reporting process is that most creditors, if not all, do not report delinquencies of less than 30 days to credit-reporting agencies. However, they may keep an internal record of the late payments.

If your payment due date has passed and you simply forgot to make the payment, again, call the credit card company immediately.

Explain that you've missed the due date (maybe you were out of town on business or had to abruptly leave due to a family emergency or medical need) and would like to make the payment immediately. Many credit card companies charge a convenience fee of up to $14.95 for processing a payment by telephone. Ask for this fee to be waived because the circumstances you encountered were beyond your control. In most instances, the representative will receive authorization from a superior to waive the transaction/convenience fee. In addition, ask for a concession to be made and for the late fee to be waived as well because you're making the payment immediately. Also, tell the representative what you will do to prevent this from occurring in the future.

If you can get both fees to be waived, you're a pretty good negotiator or you're very good at communicating. If you stink at both but manage to get both fees waived, you're doing business with an extraordinary company. If you manage to get the late fee waived but not the transaction fee, find out if you can register to pay your account online. Once you register your account online, many credit card companies will accept same-day payments without charging additional fees. This will allow you to avoid the extra charges normally associated with being late.

You can use this method with credit card companies, retailers and department store charge cards. If you're struggling to make a payment because the due date falls on a day that requires you to make multiple payments to other debtors, call one of your creditors and ask for your due date to be changed. Avoid having several accounts due at the beginning or end of the month. Creditors realize that you have other financial obligations and will normally grant your wish to change your due date.

Auto/home/personal loans

If you know that you're not going to be able to make your loan payment, again, contact the bank immediately. A number of them will try to make payment arrangements and ask when you'll be able to make the payment. If you're going to be low on funds for a few weeks, and you ask, some may even change the due date of your payment or simply waive the current payment by extending the terms of your contract. In other words, if you're scheduled to make a final payment 12 months from now, the bank will add another month, changing it to 13 months.

All of this can be done without the bank reporting a delinquency to the three credit-reporting agencies. Above all, if the terms of your loan or due date change, please request a letter from your bank stating this information. Also make sure the bank does not inadvertently report a late to the credit-reporting companies.

How to bargain with collectors

For those of you being contacted by a collection agency, the first thing I'll tell you is, "know your rights!" Next, I'll tell you to pay close attention to the information in Chapter 11, and to read the section related to collection agencies and the Fair Debt Collection Practices Act.

Collectors are very aggressive and most don't care about what's going on in your personal life. Their goal is to recover the money you owe. Once you've learned your rights when dealing with collection agencies, try to negotiate on its terms, which will probably initially begin as "pay this amount in full as soon as possible!" If the collector's demand is unreasonable, just explain that you cannot afford the proposed amount. Ask the collector to accept a settlement that is a portion of what is owed, such as 60 percent. Always start on the lower end, because the collector is sure to use a rebuttal and ask for a higher percentage.

This is when the negotiating begins. You will start low and the collector will push higher. The goal is to agree somewhere in the middle. I only recommend proposing a settlement if you are able to make the entire settlement amount in one lump payment.

Once you and the collector have decided on a reasonable settlement amount, don't pull out your check book or credit card yet!

Instead, ask the collector to draft a letter on its letterhead detailing the amount you agreed on. In addition, get the collector to agree to update your credit reports accordingly once it receives the payment (this may be to remove the debt entirely or simply report the debt as paid; it depends on what you're able to negotiate).

Receiving the letter may take as little as a few minutes or as long as several days, but it will certainly happen because the collector firmly believes it has a chance of receiving payment. If you'd like to speed up the process, provide a fax number and have the collection agency fax the settlement letter to you.

If you cannot afford to make a lump payment or cannot negotiate a lower amount, set up a payment schedule with the collector. The schedule can be weekly or monthly, citing specific dates on which you intend to make payments to the collector. The collector will probably try hard to avoid the payment plan, but fight for it. Even if you cannot identify one representative at the collection company to deal with exclusively, create your schedule and send it to the collector in writing along with your first payment. Draft a letter stating that the enclosed payment is the first of "x" amount of payments needed to repay the outstanding debt.

What you must understand about collection items is that the debts are already late and there is not much the collector can *do* to punish you as far as your credit rating is concerned. By the time an account reaches collection status, I'm almost positive that it's appearing on your credit report, so don't let a collector scare you with threats about ruining your credit record.

On the other hand, if you don't make attempts to repay, the debtor may file a judgment against you, and that may further affect your credit rating. As long as you take some steps to pay the debt, your chances of avoiding a judgment being filed against you are good. Once you create your schedule, stick to it! In the end, at least the debt will show as paid on your credit record, or it will be removed entirely.

Chapter summary

It's important to note that I'm not sharing these tips so that you can dominate or take advantage of the relationships you have with your creditors, or to teach you how to swindle collectors. There are enough personal finance books that unsuccessfully attempt to teach you that.

Bargaining with your creditors is no substitution for failing to repay what you rightfully owe or repaying your obligations on time. Knowing what you now know, you can avoid raw deals and get better ones. The truth is, overall, creditors are generally willing to negotiate, though it's not spelled out in your agreement. When determining their budgets, creditors project that they will lose a certain amount of money due to consumers' experiencing financial hardships or plain old negligence.

Though I do not believe consumers should be automatically rewarded for repaying their debts on time, creditors must recognize when consumers have displayed consistent, positive repayment patterns. They recognize these good behaviors by making some of the concessions that we've discussed: waiving late fees, changing due dates, extending terms and accepting settlements.

Creditors keep track of the amount of concessions they have made as well, such as payment arrangements, and will not make concessions to consumers who habitually have problems making payments on time. Therefore, don't abuse the relationships you have with your creditors. Hold negotiating for better terms upon the establishment of an account. Your bargaining skills should be used only when necessary; they should not become routine. To determine what new skills you've acquired from this chapter, take the following quiz.

Chapter 7—Quiz

1. Why do many consumers get stuck with bad credit contracts?

2. Creditors must run a credit check to determine the best rates available to a consumer. (True or False)

3. Normally found in credit card agreements, a _____ _____ _____ allows your credit card company to increase your rates if you fall behind on other debts.

4. If your creditor is unwilling to lower your rates after 12 months of timely payments, what are your options?

5. What types of fees may be waived if you forget to make a payment on time?

6. When offering a settlement to a collector, where should you start negotiating?

Chapter 7—Quiz Answers

1. Many consumers get stuck with bad credit contracts because they are afraid to ask for a better deal.

2. False.

3. Universal default clause.

4. If your creditor is unwilling to lower your rates after 12 months of timely payments, you may apply for a credit card with another provider and/or request that your account be closed.

5. The fees that may be waived if you forget to make a payment on time are convenience/transaction fees and late fees.

6. When offering a settlement to a collector, you should begin negotiating an amount that is 60 percent of the total balance due.

Correcting Errors on Credit Reports

How many of you have ever received a credit report that contained inaccurate personal information about you or your payment patterns to one of your debtors? It's a known fact that a significant number of credit reports contain errors, so it would behoove you to know how to correct them.

Disputing items on a credit report is a challenging task for consumers. Many are intimidated by the intricacies of credit reports, the idea of the authority of credit-reporting agencies, and the overall weight of credit records and their ability to affect various facets of living. All of these fears may be eradicated through proper education (with education comes understanding; from understanding confidence is born). In this chapter, you will learn how to properly dispute errors on your credit report.

Consumers have the right to dispute *any* portion of their credit report that is believed to be inaccurate. This right is provided in the Fair Credit Reporting Act. It is desirable but not necessary that consumers obtain copies of their credit reports from all three agencies prior to requesting a reinvestigation of inaccurate items. Doing so will save time and possibly a great deal of frustration and confusion.

Generally, the credit-reporting agencies do not share information with each other, as they are competitors. (Exceptions to this rule may exist to help protect consumers against fraud and identity theft.) In some instances, an inaccurate item may only be appearing on one or two of the three reporting agencies' records. Therefore, it would not benefit a consumer to contact a credit-reporting agency that is not reporting the error.

A consumer should focus most efforts on those credit-reporting agencies that are reporting the item erroneously. Therefore, it behooves consumers to obtain copies of their credit reports from all reporting agencies directly prior to disputing any information.

For those concerned about the length of time it takes to receive a credit report the traditional way (by writing or telephone), a new, fast alternative is accessing the Websites of the credit-reporting agencies to receive instant viewing. Of course a fee may be involved in using this method, even though a consumer may be entitled to free copies. With this method, consumers are really paying for the convenience and instant access of viewing their credit reports online.

Another reason why consumers should obtain credit reports directly from credit-reporting agencies is to receive the telephone numbers that allow them access to live operators. As explained earlier, the agencies are not legally obligated to provide live operators to consumers unless they have an exclusive copy of that reporting agency's credit report. The exclusive report (meaning it is compiled by a particular agency or pertains to one particular agency) has a confirmation or file number listed on it. These numbers are usually valid for 60–90 days ("valid" meaning they will grant consumers live access to a representative at the reporting company). The telephone systems of the credit-reporting agencies are equipped to determine if the file/ confirmation number is "valid" (meaning it belongs to the appropriate reporting agency and has been issued within the past 60–90 days). If the number is valid, the consumer will be routed to the next available customer service representative. If the number is not valid, the consumer will be routed to other prompts and forced to order a more recent copy of his or her credit report.

Consumers disputing items on their credit reports may contact credit-reporting agencies to request a reinvestigation in writing, via the World Wide Web, by fax (sometimes) or by telephone. The preferred method is writing. Doing so offers consumers a paper trail of documentation that ultimately holds credit-reporting agencies and creditors accountable for their actions, or lack thereof (in terms of correcting the errors).

All credit-reporting agencies provide a reinvestigation request form (dispute form) along with copies of disclosure credit reports. The document may be completed by consumers and sent to a credit-reporting agency to initiate a reinvestigation. The form simplifies the process in a number of ways.

First, they are printed with the consumer's file/confirmation number. This number gives employees of the reporting agency quick access to a consumer's credit record. Also, the form often contains a list of options or dispute explanations for consumers to choose from. Some examples include "never late," "account paid in full" or "account closed." Some of the forms created only allow consumers to contest elements on an account that are present at the time the report is printed. For example, if a department store account shows no history of previous late payments, the dispute option of "never late" will not be available on that particular entry.

Providing these forms to consumers helps simplify the reinvestigation process and reduce the amount of irrelevant information credit-reporting agencies typically have to comb through to find the core reason or explanation of why an entry is being disputed. As opposed to reading through pages of a typed or handwritten letter, the dispute form summarizes a research request in a few words. These forms may be photocopied if additional space is needed to address other items.

Consumers opting to submit a reinvestigation request in writing without receiving their credit reports or without using a reporting agency's reinvestigation form should compose a concise letter to the appropriate reporting company. Contrary to what most consumers believe, there is no special format for creating these letters, but it does help tremendously if they are typed.

Consumers often believe that certain wording should be included in the letters. This, too, is a fallacy. It is not necessary to quote sections of the Fair Credit Reporting Act; the credit-reporting agency already knows what its responsibilities are and what consumers' rights are. All dispute letters should contain the following information:

1. Identification:

    ◆ Complete name (maiden and married).

    ◆ All addresses used in the past five years.

    ◆ Date of birth.

    ◆ Social Security number.

2. Complete account names and numbers (if possible) of all entries being disputed.

3. A brief statement of what is inaccurate listed under or in close proximity to each contested entry.

4. Current date and signature.

5. Photocopies of one form of ID (driver's license, birth certificate, for example) and one utility bill reflecting one's current address.

6. Photocopies of any relevant documents supporting claims (for example, copies of correction letters from creditors, canceled checks or statements from creditors).

Upon completion of the letter, photocopy and file it for future reference. Consumers may wish to keep a separate file for each credit-reporting agency being contacted. These records provide reference of when the agencies were contacted and what specific items a consumer requested research on. The letter(s) should be sent to the credit-reporting agency certified mail/return receipt. This is a way of receiving proof of delivery and allows consumers to determine the exact date an agency received their letter.

This date is significant because it also begins the 30-day period a credit-reporting agency has to re-verify disputed entries. In other words, it is a very powerful tool consumers can use to ensure reporting agencies are in compliance with the 30-day re-verification time frame stipulated in the Fair Credit Reporting Act.

Some consumers may choose to request a reinvestigation via telephone. This group should be aware of the loss of accountability tools when choosing this option. As this is a verbal exchange from consumer to a credit-reporting agency employee, there is really no guarantee that a consumer has presented his or her position clearly and that the agency's employee properly investigated contested items. For example, a consumer may state that his credit card has never been delinquent. If an employee interprets this as meaning the account is paid in full, he or she has in essence mistaken the consumer's position. The consumer is actually saying his account has always been paid on time rather than that the balance has been paid in full. It is a must that consumers are certain the credit-reporting agency operator fully understands his or her position and reinvestigates entries correctly. A good way to help ensure this understanding takes place is by asking the agency's representative to summarize one's concerns at the end of the conversation.

When disputing credit entries via telephone, consumers should always document dates, times and names of representatives they speak with. If consumers possess supporting documents to substantiate their claims, they should request a fax number to submit the paperwork to a credit-reporting agency. In doing so, they may encounter some resistance from credit-reporting agency employees. Reporting agencies are often inundated with faxes and may urge frontline employees to discourage consumers from faxing documents. Consumers unable to obtain fax numbers should request a mailing address for submitting their supporting documents. The credit-reporting agency's representative should also provide an investigation confirmation number as proof that a reinvestigation has been started and as a reference tool to check the status of the reinvestigation. This number should be written on all supporting documents submitted via fax or mail as a result of the telephone conversation with a credit-reporting agency in which a reinvestigation was started. Fax transmission confirmations and notes from telephone conversations should also be filed for future reference.

Consumers receiving their credit reports online may dispute via the credit-reporting agency's Website. They will receive a confirmation number acknowledging that a reinvestigation has been started as well.

After a reinvestigation has been received and initiated from any of the aforementioned channels, the credit-reporting agency contacted may send a confirmation letter, acknowledging receipt of a consumer's request and advising them that re-verification is in progress. However, it has been my personal experience that only one of the three major credit-reporting agencies, Trans Union, sends such a letter.

Once all of the aforementioned steps have been taken and the reinvestigation is underway, sit back, relax and let the process run its course for the next 30 days. It is not necessary to call or write the agency during the reinvestigation to merely check the status or progress. Consumers should only inquire about the status if 30 days have passed and the credit-reporting agency has not responded with the results of their research. At this point, the reporting agency should be sending a letter to the consumer detailing its findings. It should also supply a consumer with an updated copy of the credit report showing the corrections made.

At the same time a credit-reporting agency is contacted to re-verify disputed credit entries, a consumer should also contact the creditor (the furnisher of the erroneous information) directly. The error should be brought to the creditor's attention and the consumer should request that a correction letter be sent to him or her, as well as to the agency reporting the incorrect information. Make sure that the letter is signed, dated, appears on the creditor's letterhead and specifically cites the error(s) and corrective action taken or requested.

Unfortunately, unless a consumer is proactive and initiates a reinvestigation, it could take up to 90 days to permanently correct the record in a reporting company's database. I am not certain why the process takes this long, but it does seem to be standard operating conditions for all of the major credit-reporting agencies and furnishers of information. Perhaps it is a reflection of antiquated operating systems that suffer from a lack of technology, but I'm not sure. Once the consumer receives the correction letter, he or she should forward a copy directly to the agency reporting the data.

If a credit-reporting agency does not respond with results of a reinvestigation, a consumer should call immediately to determine the cause of the delay. In some cases, the agency may have completed the case but not notified a consumer due to a discrepancy with the address (a missing apartment number, wrong city or zip code, for example). On the other hand, if a reporting agency inadvertently failed to re-verify an entry that was contested by a consumer, it has also shifted the upper hand to the consumer.

The Fair Credit Reporting Act only allows reporting agencies 30 days to complete its reinvestigation, unless it receives other relevant information during the reinvestigation. In this case the reinvestigation may be extended for an additional 15 days. If an agency fails to complete the reinvestigation in the above time frame, it has violated federal law. This violation holds a credit-reporting agency accountable for damages a consumer may have incurred as a result of its negligence. In addition, willful noncompliance of a reporting agency is punishable by law.

The first action a consumer should take is contacting the Federal Trade Commission and filing a complaint against the offending credit-reporting agency. This may be done via telephone, online or via email:

Phone: (877) ftc-help

Online: *www.ftc.gov*

Mail: Federal Trade Commission—crc

600 Pennsylvania Avenue NW

Washington, DC 20580

The Federal Trade Commission will provide a complaint number to the consumer as proof that it has recorded the concern. It is paramount that consumers contact the Federal Trade Commission and report violations because if enough complaints are received, then it may begin its own investigation to determine the validity of the claims. In the past (January 2000), the three major credit-reporting agencies paid a combined $2.5 million dollars in penalties for not complying with provisions of the Fair Credit Reporting Act that required them to have live phone representatives available during normal business hours. Charges alleged that the credit-reporting agencies knowingly blocked millions of calls from consumers seeking to discuss possible mistakes on their credit reports. It also alleged that the agencies forced many consumers to endure excruciatingly lengthy hold times. These facts came into fruition due in large part to the amount of complaints made to the Federal Trade Commission by consumers. For this reason alone, it is important that consumer channel their complaints to the Federal Trade Commission.

After the complaint is filed, the credit-reporting agency should be contacted and provided with the complaint number. The consumer that has carefully documented his or her correspondence with a reporting company in writing via mail has the most leverage here. The return receipt proves that the request was received by an agency and also confirms the date of receipt. This is a very powerful tool that can carry substantial weight in court (in the unlikely event that the issue is not amicably resolved). Upon contacting the credit-reporting agency, the consumer should demand that the ignored items be expunged or updated immediately.

Consumers may encounter resistance on all fronts; this should be expected. They must not let the frontline employee disprove the validity of their claim. The fact remains that the credit-reporting agency did not complete the reinvestigation in the time stipulated by law. Further, the consumer has proof that the agency received the request and the date it was received. Do not hesitate to advise the credit-reporting agency employee of this fact.

Listen up and listen closely! At this point, the agency's representative will probably offer to begin the reinvestigation on items that were previously ignored. Don't accept the offer, even if an expedited (rush) case is offered. The bottom line is the agency has 30 days to complete its reinvestigation. Not 35, not 31, not 30 days and five minutes, but 30 days. And consumers should make the credit-reporting agency honor and respect the law.

The only exception that applies is if a consumer provides the agency with additional, relevant information related to the claim during the course of the investigation.

If a consumer's request to have the ignored credit entries investigated is not honored by the frontline employee, the consumer should escalate to the next level. Ask to speak with a supervisor. If the supervisor does not comply, address the issue with a manager.

Consumers must hold firm and stand their ground. I recommend escalating to the highest level possible, even if that means sifting through the consumer affairs layers (which often includes a group of seasoned, tenured employees) and, ultimately, reaching the chief executive officer or other executive at the credit-reporting agency. Do it! It will not be easy, but the agency will respect a consumer's tenacity and confidence. In addition, they would much rather comply with a consumer's request than risk an ugly battle in which their negligence is exposed and they are forced to pay fines for federal violations and damages.

In the unlikely event that the credit-reporting agency does not comply, the consumer should seriously consider seeking legal advice and exploring litigation with a reputable attorney, especially if one has suffered financial damages. These intentions should also be conveyed clearly to the credit-reporting agency (in writing) with complete resolution requirements. Also, the consumer should advise that he or she has filed a formal complaint with the Federal Trade Commission. Consumers should be clear about the seriousness of the incident and avoid settling for less than what is fair to them and required by the credit-reporting agency.

What to do if a reinvestigation does not resolve the dispute

If a credit-reporting agency's research concludes that an entry will remain unchanged because it has been confirmed to be accurate by the furnisher, the consumer should go directly to the creditor who is providing the agency with the erroneous information and demand corrective action immediately. This is with the understanding that the entry being reported is inaccurate, not just that it's negative and a consumer wishes to have it removed. The burden of responsibility now lies solely on the creditor to correct the mistake, because the reporting agency has fulfilled its legal obligation of re-verifying the entry.

Consumers must understand that not all of the errors rest on credit-reporting agencies, but furnishers as well. In addition, if a creditor's negligence in this process causes a consumer to incur hardship, it has to answer for its actions or lack thereof.

The Fair Credit Reporting Act also applies both to creditors and any other furnisher of information to credit-reporting agencies. This means that they can legally be held liable for their part in failing to correct erroneous information and/or knowingly furnishing such data to credit-reporting agencies.

Thanks to amendments made to the Fair Credit Reporting Act, once a consumer notifies a furnisher of an error, similar to credit-reporting agencies, it has 30 days to reinvestigate and correct the mistake. Consumers may also seek restitution for damages suffered as a result of a creditor's negligence and noncompliance of the Fair Credit Reporting Act. Please refer to the sample letters available in the appendix for help getting started with submitting a reinvestigation request to the credit-reporting agencies and your creditors.

Chapter summary

The credit reinvestigation process has a fair share of obstacles for all parties involved. For consumers, knowing their rights and how to exercise those rights helps to level the playing field. They should not become discouraged or intimidated by a notion of the ultimate authority of credit-reporting agencies and creditors. Rather, they should defend their liberties and hold these organizations accountable for complying with legal mandates.

Knowledge of those rights and laws arms and empowers consumers with the tools necessary to protect them from mistreatment. In addition, consumers who understand how to correct errors on their credit records are less likely to consult or seek the assistance of unscrupulous credit doctors that typically inflict harm on consumers. These professionals often fall short of promises and charge consumers hefty fees for their services.

Disputing inaccuracies on one's credit report is an action that all consumers can take for themselves. In theory, the process is straightforward. In reality, however, it has developed into one that consumers detest (due in part to processes and procedures of those that furnish and report information).

Though resolving errors may not be completely hassle-free, consumers can lessen potential negative impacts by properly documenting information and remaining organized.

Correcting errors on credit reports is a process that leads consumers to steady interaction with credit-reporting agencies and creditors. Thus, it is paramount that consumers know what to say and how to communicate when contacting these entities for the purpose of promptly resolving an issue.

The following page contains a quiz on the dispute process. Please take a few minutes to complete it and determine how much information you have retained from the current chapter. Try answering the questions from memory, but review the chapter if help is needed. Good luck!

Chapter 8—Quiz

1. Do the national credit-reporting agencies normally share data with each other?

2. When disputing, the best way to contact a credit-reporting agency is by _____ because it _____ and _____.

3. Are consumers required to have a credit report in order to dispute erroneous information on their credit records?

4. What type of information should be documented when having a telephone conversation with a credit-reporting agency employee?

5. How long should a reinvestigation take to be completed by a credit-reporting agency or creditor?

6. Complaints concerning noncompliance of credit laws should be directed to the _____ _____ _____.

Chapter 8—Quiz Answers

1. The national credit-reporting agencies normally do not share data with each other.

2. When disputing, the best way to contact a credit-reporting agency is by writing because it provides proof that an agency received a request and establishes a documentation trail.

3. Consumers are not required to have a credit report in order to dispute erroneous information.

4. The date, time and names of employees should be documented when conversing with credit-reporting agencies.

5. A reinvestigation should take no more than 30 days to be completed by a credit-reporting agency.

6. Complaints concerning noncompliance of credit laws should be directed to the Federal Trade Commission.

Restoring Credit Through Consumer Counseling

Finding a credible credit counselor

In recent years, credit-counseling services have grown increasingly popular. Commercials and advertisements flood television, radio and even the information superhighway. Credit experts appear on local and national media networks and never fail to mention the benefits of consumer credit counseling. Many consumers telephone and write credit-reporting agencies seeking information about credit counseling services. Consumers want to know how to get creditors off their backs, how paying debts through such an agency affects their ability to obtain credit in the future and what is involved (and what costs are incurred) in consolidating debts.

Unfortunately, most consumers do not inquire about credit counseling until they have acquired a substantial amount of debt and fallen severely behind on their payments. In some cases they are so delinquent that credit counseling may no longer be an option for salvaging their debts. Let's discuss the dynamics of credit counselors, their value and the key factors about this topic that usually escape consumers and cause frustration.

Most major cities have consumer credit-counseling service offices. Traditionally known as CCCSs, these offices generally operate under the name of the city in which they are located. For example, a credit-counseling center in Memphis, Tennessee, may be known as Consumer Credit Counseling Services of Memphis. However, in many instances, they may not be affiliated with the city in which they are located. Most, if not all, are nonprofit organizations that offer money-management education, home-buying/mortgage education, credit and debt counseling and debt management programs, which critics may argue is the organization's bread and butter.

The mother company of the most reputable credit-counseling agencies is the National Foundation for Credit Counseling (NFCC). This is a national network that currently offers credit-counseling services in more than 1,300 locations throughout the United States.

It is strongly recommended that consumers seeking credit counseling make sure the office they are working with is a member of the National Foundation for Credit Counseling. Offices affiliated with this network have counselors that undergo training in the area of credit and debt management. Once the training has been completed, the counselors have undergone assessments to gauge their understanding of finances and counseling, and they even receive certification.

In addition to having highly skilled counselors, each member location of the National Foundation for Credit Counseling receives accreditation by an independent third-party organization, called the Council on Accreditation for Children and Family Services. Consumers would be wise to inquire as to whether a credit-counseling agency has affiliations with the National Foundation for Credit Counseling due to the benefits offered through such a relationship.

More helpful information about selecting a credit counselor or debt-management firm may be obtained by visiting the Federal Trade Commission's Website at *http://www.ftc.gov/credit*.

Use standards to choose a credit counselor

For the past few years, the credit-counseling industry has experienced a substantial amount of growth. A number of debt-relief organizations have even taken to tactics such as telemarketing and e-mail spamming to advertise and market their products and services to consumers. The proliferation of credit counseling-type businesses has grown so rapidly that it has gotten difficult to determine the credible and reputable from the unscrupulous and misleading.

Some consumers have experienced less than acceptable service from many of these agencies and have been quite expressive with their complaints. Some credit-counseling businesses have been accused of muscling consumers into debt-management programs prematurely, without carefully analyzing their financial situations or providing educational assistance.

Additionally, some of these providers have allegedly assessed fees prior to rendering services and charged fees where unnecessary. Local and national media outlets have broadcasted several reports exposing the iniquities and shortcomings of many credit-counseling agencies and have painted them as incredulous, expedient organizations that take advantage of consumers by partnering with credit grantors.

Talk and news concerning the abuses levied on consumers by various credit-counseling agencies even caught the attention of some government personnel. So much so that some have echoed the need for their intervention by creating laws to regulate the industry.

As a result of these factors, and more specifically those adversely impacting creditors, the advisory council of the National Foundation for Credit Counseling assembled in 2003 to assess the current situation of the industry and acknowledge many opportunities for improvement.

Though triggered most by incessant consumer complaints, negative media coverage and decreased contributions, the National Foundation for Credit Counseling took important steps in identifying gaps and addressing them without being ordered to do so by the federal government. To this degree, they were proactive.

The primary goal of the advisory council was to identify and *suggest* standards in the credit-counseling industry to assist in protecting consumers from mistreatment. Inasmuch as all parties involved in the industry (creditors and counseling agencies) would be encouraged to adopt and adhere to these best practices, they are not required to.

The advisory council developed a list of commendable guidelines for member agencies and creditors. Some of the highlights worthy of mentioning include:

- All member agency counselors are to be certified through an approved program.

- Member agencies are to be governed by a board of independent directors representing the community the agency serves.

- Protection of client's funds.

- Member agencies are to maintain reasonable fees for their counsel or services.

- Member agencies are prohibited from paying commissions to counselors and other employees in order to help prevent conflicts of interest.

- Member agencies are required to respond to consumer complaints within five business days and attempt to resolve the issue.

- Creditors are to make reasonable rate/fee concessions to assist consumers in debt-relief resources.

- Creditors are to discontinue collection efforts while consumers are working with a credit-counseling agency.

- Creditors are to accurately report account information to credit-reporting agencies.

- Creditors are to respond to consumer complaints within five business days.

This list is not inclusive and many more proposals were included in the advisory council's suggested standards.

Ideally, all member agencies and contributing creditors would accept and adhere to the proposed standards of the National Foundation for Credit Counseling. The council's member quality standards for accreditation are said to include the best practices derived from the advisory council's efforts in 2003.

One of the goals the advisory council had was to create standards that could serve as a litmus test to distinguish the good credit-counseling agencies from the bad ones, with the hope that state governments will create and enforce laws supporting the prescribed standards. In this sense, state governments would use the standards of the council as a benchmark for consumers to use in measuring the best counseling agencies to seek advice from, and possibly recommend those to consumers seeking debt-management assistance.

The credit-counseling industry is mostly unregulated by the federal government, unlike the credit-reporting industry. In fact, the Fair Credit Reporting Act does not even mention the credit-counseling industry.

If consumer complaints about the abusive and deceptive practices of some credit-counseling companies continue to increase and the industry members do not fully comply with the standards proposed by the National Foundation for Credit Counseling, intervention by the federal government is inevitable.

While the standards created serve as a solid foundation for the credit-counseling industry, it's uncertain that they will do much to turn around its debilitating reputation among consumers and as portrayed in the media. The most important factor regarding the inception and implementation of the standards is enforcement; because there is none.

Any of the members, agencies and creditors may or may not adhere to the standards created and suggested by the National Foundation for Credit Counseling. Compliance is completely voluntary. There is no system of checks and balances that would ensure all of the duties proposed by the standards are fully executed. Further, there are no consequences for those who choose to violate the standards.

For these reasons, the National Foundation for Credit Counseling may not realize the success it set out to accomplish. Our government is successful because of the system of checks and balances. Our households are orderly because they operate under rules of enforcement as well, with parents holding their children accountable to complying with house rules. Without rules and application of them, our homes would be in complete disarray, complete chaos even.

Unfortunately, the National Foundation for Credit Counseling is not in a position to issue mandates for creditors and member agencies. Because it is a nonprofit organization that relies heavily on support from creditors, it's not in its best interest to try to force compliance of its standards. Doing so will further exacerbate already fledging contributions that the credit-counseling industry is facing.

On the other hand, making adherence to the standards optional may allow members to continue exhibiting questionable actions and behavior toward consumers. Theoretically, the standards may not induce positive effects because they have no enforcing element. In the meantime, it will be interesting to observe the fate of the credit-counseling industry. Will members adopt the standards composed by the National Foundation for Credit Counseling and drive the consumer complaints down, or will some continue unethical practices, forcing more complaints, negative media coverage and tainted reputations?

Consumer credit counseling offers an alternative to filing bankruptcy and, if followed closely, helps consumers gain control and successfully manage their debt. Upon contacting a credit-counseling center in the National Foundation for Credit Counseling's network, consumers can expect to receive a detailed review of their financial status. Financial components that are carefully considered include debt, income, assets and liabilities. If warranted, based upon the analysis of a consumer's financial standing, a debt-management plan may be created. Otherwise, counseling may be offered and function just as effectively in getting a consumer's finances under control.

The services offered under the network are relatively inexpensive. If a consumer's debt and financial condition require a debt-management plan, depending upon the amount of debt owed, it could take three to five years to complete the repayment of funds to creditors. Through this plan, consumers make periodic deposits to the credit-counseling agency (usually monthly), and the agency will in turn disburse the money to creditors. In some cases, the agency may be able to get creditor fees and charges waived for consumers. There is no guarantee, however, that such additional costs will not be assessed. Some agencies may even be able to have rates reduced on higher-interest credit cards over time.

Debt-management programs can be effective in reducing consumer debt and helping them manage credit wisely. These benefits may be reaped if the participant is disciplined enough to adhere to the program. However, participating in a debt-management plan does have an impact upon a consumer's creditworthiness.

Consumers should not be led into thinking that such plans come at no cost to their credit standing. While debt-management programs may offset late payments, creditors included in the repayment plan will report to credit-reporting agencies that the account is being paid through a financial counseling plan. Such a statement will be attached to the account when it is electronically reported to credit-reporting agencies. Unfortunately, this statement could indicate to future, potential creditors that a consumer needed third-party assistance to ensure that his or her financial obligations were repaid to debtors.

Now that you are an expert on credit scoring, you know that such a comment could trigger an adverse reading by scoring models. Newer scoring models may include enhancements that ignore these statements. But, for lenders, it is expensive to purchase and implement software containing the updates. In order to limit costs associated in uploading new software, many lenders continue to conduct business using the original scoring product that was purchased. Thus, older scoring models will pick up "financial counseling indicators" and factor them into the credit score.

Many consumers are surprised to receive declination letters after completing a debt-management program. This is because they are not initially informed of the potential impact these plans may have on their abilities to obtain credit in the future. Such unknowns lead to consumer frustration and sometimes anger. The facts, whether positive or negative, should be revealed to consumers up front, but I don't imagine all credit-counseling agency employees are aware of all potential impacts either.

Keep in mind, I have not provided these details to deter enrollment with credit-counseling programs, but so that those considering know the truth about all factors that may affect their credit. Any consumer considering a debt-management program should ask how his or her involvement in the program could impact their creditworthiness. Be weary of *any* organization that emphatically denies a debt-management program will affect one's credit standing.

In the end, consumers must weigh their options carefully and make the best decision for themselves based upon personal circumstances. Consumers should explore their options by thoroughly investigating possible outcomes; asking many questions, seeking facts so that they can understand the consequences and by making informed, intelligent decisions based on all this. In my opinion, it would not be wise for consumers to rule out credit-counseling assistance based upon the fact that it could trigger a lower credit score.

However, when enrolling in a debt-management plan, consumers should avoid applying for new credit. The goal is to become debt-free, or at least learn how to better manage debt, and not continue with negative credit behavior.

Many credit-counseling organizations have ties with creditors. Because these agencies are nonprofit companies and do not rely heavily on small payments (if any) paid to them by consumers, an obvious question arises: "How do they remain afloat financially?" Creditors affiliated with credit-counseling agencies often provide the majority of funding. Creditors voluntarily give a percentage of money acquired through debt-management programs to the credit-counseling agency.

Thus, an important relationship exits between the two entities. Credit-counseling agencies help creditors secure repayment of debts and creditors pay them for their service. Credit-counseling centers may be viewed as third-party negotiators in this context.

Chapter summary

Consumers who are not as gifted in reaching alternative agreements with debtors or salvaging their creditworthiness simultaneously may find credit-counseling services of valuable interest. As demonstrated by the recent growth in credit-counseling businesses, some may not hold themselves to high ethical standards; in which case, consumers tend to suffer.

Any consumer considering or seeking the assistance of a consumer credit-counseling agency will reduce their chances of experiencing inadequate service by asking the appropriate questions. Though not guaranteed to eliminate unwanted problems, when reviewing credit-counseling agencies, determining if they meet certain standards could prove beneficial.

More information about consumer credit counseling may be obtained by visiting the Website of the National Foundation for Credit Counseling at *www.nfcc.org*. They may also be contacted at 1-800-388-2227 to determine the location of the nearest network office in your area.

Chapter 9—Quiz

1. Consumer credit counseling is an alternative to _____ .

2. References to consumer credit counseling on one's credit report do not affect a consumer's ability to obtain credit. (True/False)

3. How are credit-counseling organizations paid?

4. Consumer credit-counseling services have to comply with the Fair Credit Reporting Act. (True/False)

Chapter 9—Quiz Answers

1. Consumer credit counseling is an alternative to filing bankruptcy.

2. False.

3. Credit-counseling organizations are paid mostly by contributions of creditors.

4. False.

Avoiding Identity Theft andFraud: Reclaiming Your Status

Social Security numbers and protecting your privacy

T he uses of Social Security numbers today are vast. Everyone from doctors to universities request them. But what is the reason for this?

Many of us never bother to challenge these parties or even ask why such a personal and fragile piece of information is needed to conduct normal business. How freely do you provide your personal information? Do you safeguard your social security at all costs? We are issued Social Security numbers by the Social Security Administration to keep an account of our income and for the purpose of receiving benefits. How is it, then, that our Social Security numbers are used for various other reasons?

I would argue that credit grantors and various service providers were probably pioneers in the movement to use Social Security numbers to keep track of or verify consumers' financial histories and records.

Today, one of the first questions lenders and services providers ask on applications for credit is: "What is your Social Security number?" The credit application and credit-reporting processes alike rely heavily on Social Security numbers to identify and track financial records. In fact, without having an applicant's Social Security number, credit grantors may experience significant risks and setbacks.

For example, it would be difficult to obtain positive matches when attempting to access consumer credit reports without Social Security numbers. Ideally, the identification supplied on a credit application (name, address and date of birth, and so on) should match the ID information of the credit report that is accessed.

However, there are millions of names and addresses stored in the databases of credit-reporting agencies. Add the anomalies of consumers constantly changing their addresses and names or consumers using variations of their names (for example, Bill versus William) and it becomes even more difficult for lenders to secure an exact match.

The only identifier that is constant and unique to an individual consumer is their Social Security number. This is important because credit grantors need to review the right credit record in order to make sound decisions to extend or deny credit. It is also important because they would be violating federal law by accessing the credit record of a consumer that did not give authorization to review his or her credit history.

The same concept holds true when creditors are furnishing account information to credit-reporting agencies about their customers. An exact match is needed or the dangerous possibility of an account being attached to the wrong credit record is present. This is often how incorrect data makes its way onto consumers' credit reports. The greatest opportunity for credit-reporting agencies and furnishers is to ensure the right information is attached to the appropriate credit record by utilizing Social Security numbers.

Considering this process, our credit system has become virtually dependent on the Social Security numbers of consumers. Though it would likely be difficult to obtain credit from most companies without providing a Social Security number, it is not completely impossible to do.

Legally, nothing prohibits companies from requesting such information and lenders may legitimately deny credit based upon their inability to verify a consumer's credit history. In addition, most student loans even list the students' Social Security numbers as a portion of the account number. If you have any student loans appearing on your credit report, I urge you to take a closer look at it. They're almost guaranteed to contain your Social Security numbers.

The greatest challenge faced by all of these entities is protecting illegitimate access to consumers' Social Security numbers. Because our Social Security numbers are being used for purposes other than what they were designed for and stored in the systems of various companies, they are extremely vulnerable. It is easier to control access to and protect such information when it is managed in a single database. In a world driven by cutting-edge technology, it is not hard for thieves to identify resources that will penetrate even the most advanced, secure databases.

There are times when "system glitches, failures and errors" are cited for causing consumers' personal information to be exposed and compromised. In most of these instances, affected consumers will receive letters informing them of such occurrences and urging them to take measures to protect their personal information, up to and including contacting credit-reporting agencies to request a fraud alert and credit report.

As fraud and identity theft continues to pose threats to consumers, it is safe to assume that lenders and various other institutions that use and store consumers' personal information will be required to assume more responsibility for protecting the data. It's not a consumer's fault that a "glitch" resulted in his or her personal information being exposed.

To completely alter the way consumers' Social Security numbers are used requires a strong demand. Consumers are going to have to challenge creditors, employers and various service providers regarding the use of their Social Security numbers. If the use is not related to taxes, income or benefits, consumers must begin to voice opposition, forcing these businesses to find alternate methods of conducting business.

One creative solution is to replace use of consumers' Social Security numbers with another unique identifier (numeric or alphanumeric). However, history shows that a change of this magnitude will require involvement of two very important groups: a well-organized contingency of consumers and the government (in particular the Federal Trade Commission). The need already exists, and as fraud and identity theft grows, so will the demand.

Consumers may increase the demand at a number of levels. Write letters or call your local representatives and state attorney general's office. Voice your concerns to the FTC. Most importantly, let your creditors, employers, universities and various other users of your information know how you feel and firmly demand change.

Definition of fraud and identity theft

Though often related, fraud and identity theft have slightly different meanings. *The American Heritage Dictionary* defines "fraud" as a deception deliberately practiced in order to obtain an unfair or unlawful gain. Let's look at an example of fraud on a very basic level:

Sally is leaving the local mall after a couple hours of shopping. As she approaches her car in the parking garage, a stranger notices her with quite a few bags in her hands and nears with a sales offer. The stranger offers Sally a brand-new multimedia device for only $100.

After reviewing the box, Sally is excited. It's just the model she wanted, and for $100 it's a great deal! Sally pays the stranger and receives the merchandise in exchange.

When she gets home to try out her brand-new electronic equipment, she is livid to discover two bricks inside the box as opposed to the media player she thought she was getting. Sally has been a victim of fraud.

This is the classic example that we've all seen on our local news channels, right? Identity theft, on the other hand, is the unauthorized use of another's identifying information (name, address, Social Security number, date of birth, and so on) for personal gain by establishing accounts or services or by making purchases. Identity theft is best classified as a "type of fraud" that usually involves one's credit and financial information.

Let's say Sally accidentally left her driver's license and credit card at the counter of the department store she recently visited. When she returns to the store (about two hours later), both her driver's license and credit card are gone and the cashier has not see them.

Sally immediately notifies her credit card issuer and cancels the line of credit. Four weeks later, Sally requests a copy of her credit report from Experian and notices two new accounts that were opened within the past month, each carrying high balances. In addition, there is a substantial amount of creditor inquiries listed. The inquiries indicate that applications for credit have been submitted in her name.

Upon further investigation, Sally learns that the two new accounts were opened the same week that she lost her driver's license and credit card (which were never recovered). Sally has been a victim of identity theft because unauthorized accounts were opened in her name using her identification.

If the lost credit card had been used to make unauthorized purchases, Sally would have also been a victim of credit card fraud. Credit fraud, tax fraud and identity theft are almost always inseparable.

Identity theft and fraud facts

The Identity Theft Clearinghouse is an identity theft database launched in November 1999 by the Federal Trade Commission. The purpose of this repository is to collect consumer complaints about fraud and identity theft and assign particular cases to law enforcement for legal action as necessary. It is a database that stores consumer identity theft concerns received via their Website or toll-free telephone number.

To optimize the information contained in the database, access has been granted to law enforcement agencies to identify trends and ingenious techniques employed by identity thieves to ruin consumers' credit. Complaint data that may reveal credit-reporting agencies' and creditors' negligence in safeguarding consumers' identities is shared so that their leaders may review their procedures and implement more effective, secure guidelines.

The other pertinent information shared with this sector is consumers' experiences in getting outstanding credit entries resulting from identity theft resolved; particularly, those in which victims encountered difficulty with a credit-reporting agency or creditor while trying to absolve themselves from responsibility of accounts established fraudulently.

Consumers who have been victims of identity theft have expressed challenges faced when contacting both credit-reporting agencies and creditors to resolve fraudulent data that has been appended to their credit records.

Traditionally, consumers claim they do not receive proper assistance over the telephone when contacting credit-reporting agencies and, further, believe they are reluctant to reinvestigate or remove incorrect information from their credit records.

Lenders of credit do not escape consumer complaints either. Victims often accuse creditors of reporting fraudulent information to credit-reporting agencies and attempting to collect on debts even after consumers notify them that the account(s) resulted from unauthorized use of their identities. In addition, consumers claim that issuers of credit are reluctant to or fail to cancel accounts opened fraudulently. Furthermore, they insist that creditors are slow to correct unauthorized charges made on legitimately established accounts that do belong to them.

Consumers must acknowledge that they are vulnerable to becoming victims of identity theft, more so today than ever before. This awareness is the first step in protecting one's identity. Growing use of the Internet to make credit-related transactions has provided a convenient method of doing business on one hand; on the other, it has further exacerbated consumers' confidence that their personal information is secure.

Identity theft is a major source of consumer frustration and is one of the fastest growing crimes in the United States, with the number of reported victims multiplying at a steady rate. Consider the data from the Identity Theft Clearinghouse that was collected for 2002 and 2003. The popularity and widespread use of the Internet offers another avenue for criminals to steal consumers' identities, but by no means represent an exclusive method for crooks. Criminals, particularly identity thieves, are relentless in discovering innovative, clever schemes to secure a consumer's personal information.

The Identity Theft Clearinghouse's data shows that 42 percent of consumers that reported identity theft in 2002 were victims of credit card fraud. The majority of them had new accounts opened in their names, while others experienced unauthorized charges on existing accounts.

The next largest area where consumers were targeted is telecommunications and utility fraud. Of victims, 22 percent had telecommunication or utility services activated in their identities. The most popular service that identity thieves took advantage of was wireless telecommunication.

Bank fraud comprised 17 percent of all reports of fraud, with the leading type being unauthorized checks written in a consumer's name. Victims in this category also reported that new accounts (checking and savings) were established in their identities and unauthorized electronic withdrawals had occurred on existing accounts.

Some victims (9 percent) even reported that their identities had been used for securing employment.

Fraudulent loans (student, personal, business, home and auto) accounted for 6 percent of consumers' frustrations in 2002.

Lastly, 8 percent of victims reported that government benefits or legal documents had been obtained in their identities, including driver's licenses and Social Security cards. A small percentage even had fraudulent tax returns filed in their names.

Other consequences consumers endured were wrongful criminal records, unauthorized medical services, Internet-access accounts, residential leases, bankruptcies and security/investment purchases or trades.

In 2003, credit card fraud resulting from identity theft was again identified as the most common type among consumers that reported being victimized. It accounted for 33 percent of all reported fraud.

Following credit card fraud was telecommunication and utility fraud at 22 percent. According to similar data reported in 2002, wireless products (mobile phones, for example) lead this category.

Bank fraud remained the same, employment fraud increased to 11 percent and fraud related to government benefits and legal documents resulted in 8 percent of consumers' frustrations.

Unauthorized loans rose to 8 percent in 2003, and the miscellaneous fraud that occurred increased from less than 10 percent in 2002, to a record 19 percent in 2003.

In both years, the channel used to commit the majority of fraudulent transactions was the Internet (45 percent in 2002 and 55 percent in 2003).

Consumers targeted the most are 18 to 49 year olds (accounting for 70 percent of ID theft and fraud reported in 2003). This group was followed by those aged 50 and up (accounting for 23 percent of ID theft and fraud in 2003). Minors (under 18 years of age) composed 3 percent of all reported identity theft and fraud. These numbers are almost identical to those from 2002.

The various types of fraud reported in 2002 and 2003 may total more than 100 percent because some consumers reported being victims in multiple categories. The two obvious trends from the data are:

◆   The use of the Internet to steal consumers' identities and commit acts of fraud is steadily increasing. This is likely related to the fact that consumers use the Internet to make the majority of their financial transactions. With personal finacial data being placed on the World Wide Web, there is a significant increase in the chances of a consumer falling victim to identity theft.

♦ The fact that the miscellaneous category catapulted to 19 percent of all reported fraud indicates that thieves are becoming more creative with how they use consumers' personal and financial information. Reported credit card fraud resulting from identity theft decreased from 42 percent in 2002 to 33 percent in 2003. Where credit card fraud had the sharpest decrease, various forms of fraud covered in the miscellaneous category had the largest increase.

Identity thieves use a number of techniques to achieve their goals. The majority of consumers who become victims of ID theft do not know how their personal information was obtained. The truth is, gaining access to consumers' personal information is not difficult. Listing the techniques crooks use is not the most effective way to prevent the crime from occurring. In fact, there may not be a way to completely prevent identity theft, but consumers may curtail it by staying informed.

What to do if you are a victim of identity theft or fraud

Now that some fundamental facts have been disclosed regarding identity theft, be prepared so that you know what actions to take if you become a victim. First, contact each of the credit-reporting agencies and have fraud alerts placed on your credit records. This will help curtail the possibility of unauthorized accounts being opened in your identity. The fraud departments of the three national credit-reporting agencies are:

Equifax: 1-800-525-6285

Experian: 1-888-397-3742

Trans Union: 1-800-680-7289

These numbers may be automated or they may offer an option to speak with a representative. If the latter is presented as an option, you may be able to receive additional, pertinent information pertaining to your credit record, such as the most recent credit inquiries made, any new accounts opened and any new addresses appearing on your credit report.

Unfortunately, consumers may not be able to receive a complete verbal disclosure of their credit records over the telephone. If consumers are lucky enough to speak with a customer service representative, it is more important that they are informed of recent activity appearing on their credit reports than for them inquire about every detail. This is based on the idea that the recent occurrences are most likely going to reveal the extent of damage that has been done resulting from identity theft.

After the alert has been added, which is normally within minutes of the request, the credit-reporting agency will automatically send a hard copy of a consumer's credit report to him or her. In addition, the first credit reporting agency contacted will notify the other two major reporting agencies.

While waiting to receive the physical copy of the credit report, a consumer should contact his or her local law enforcement office and file a police report citing identity theft and/or fraud. Names and account numbers (if possible) of all entries confirmed to have been established fraudulently should be included on the report. Having more details about the accounts will aid tremendously in helping to have the fraudulent items expunged from your credit record. Any addresses associated with the unauthorized account(s) should also be listed in the police report. Obtain a copy of the police report for your records as well.

Next, log on to *www.consumer.gov/idtheft/affidavit.htm* or call 1-877-438-4338. Consumers may download the new Identity Theft Affidavit form. This standard form provides uniformity among credit-reporting agencies and various creditors to be informed of new, unauthorized accounts opened in consumers' identities.

This form should be completed as meticulously as possible and sent via mail (certified with return receipt) to each credit-reporting agency and creditor with a record of an unauthorized account. Attach a photocopy of the police report, at least two legal identification documents (driver's license or birth certificate, for example), and a succinct letter detailing your request for prompt action leading to resolution. The letter should also ask that you receive written confirmation of investigation results and be specifically addressed to the fraud departments of each company contacted.

The importance of police reports

Police reports play a vital role in helping to absolve consumers of responsibility for fraudulent charges and accounts established through identity theft. In fact, there are some states that have adopted laws requiring credit-reporting agencies to promptly block items appearing on consumer credit reports resulting from identity theft. Some states with these laws include Alabama, California, Colorado and Washington. When a consumer has been a victim of identity theft and accounts have been established as a result of the theft, he or she must have all of those accounts listed in the police report.

Upon receipt of a relevant, valid police report, court order or department of motor vehicle investigative report, a credit-reporting agency must promptly block the items listed and notify the furnisher of the information that the item has been blocked.

The items listed in the appropriate report will be blocked permanently unless: (1) a consumer misrepresents information in the report, (2) a consumer believes an item was blocked in error, (3) a credit-reporting agency believes (in good faith and reasonable judgment) that a consumer has knowingly received goods, services or monies resulting from a block that was added under false pretenses or misrepresentation of facts or (4) a credit-reporting agency receives a subsequent court order that issued the original block request. If a block is lifted or a previously deleted item is reinserted, the credit-reporting agency is required to notify a consumer of such action in writing.

Regardless of whether or not consumers are residents of one of the aforementioned states, filing a police report with local authorities is imperative, and it should still be submitted to credit-reporting agencies and creditors when identity theft has occurred. Most of the credit-reporting agencies will recognize valid police reports from all states. To determine if the state in which you reside has enacted special consumer protection laws regarding identity theft and its relationship with credit, visit *www.cornell.edu/topics/state_statutes.html*.

Identity theft insurance

Due to the proliferation of identity theft and fraud, many insurance providers are offering ID theft insurance to consumers. Creditors and consumer-reporting agencies alike are capitalizing on the public's interest in preventing fraud or identity theft by offering monitoring services. These useful services allow subscribers to receive frequent copies of their credit reports and/or notifications of recent activity. One major credit-reporting agency even offers identity theft insurance as a part of its monitoring package.

Identity theft insurance may be purchased for as little as $25 per policy. The policies usually cover monies lost while trying to resolve unauthorized accounts. They include reimbursement for telephone calls, mailing costs, legal fees and lost wages.

The amount of money reimbursed for lost wages may have a cap. Make sure this figure is identified in a policy prior to signing the contract with a provider.

Most require a deductible, some as much as $500. While identity theft insurance covers the costs consumers incur while trying to correct their credit records, it does not safeguard the actual credit record, nor does it repair it. Unfortunately, consumers are still stuck with that onerous task.

Critics of identity theft insurance often focus on this point. They would like identity theft insurance to mirror other types of insurance, such as homeowner's and auto, which repair the actual damages.

However, consumer credit reports are not real property; they don't become tangible until the content is retrieved from a database and printed on paper. Still, opponents believe the insurance should repair the damages done to credit reports, not just reimburse consumers for the time and money it takes them to correct the fraudulent information.

Identity theft insurance provides $15,000–$25,000 of coverage on average. Though some opponents of identity theft insurance may think the coverage is inadequate, for a small price it is a great investment. First, the insurance may not repair actual damages but it alleviates most costs associated in notifying the furnishers and reporters (creditors and consumer-reporting agencies, respectively) of erroneous, fraudulent information.

The legal burden of correcting the inaccurate data is the responsibility of creditors and the reporting agencies, not insurance providers or consumers. These prior two entities have a legal obligation to do their part in correcting mistakes. Consumers' only responsibility is notifying these two parties of the errors.

Other detractors of identity theft insurance contend that the likelihood of consumers becoming a victim of identity theft is so small that purchasing such a policy is a waste of money. However, with payouts being as much as $25,000, it can be a wonderful return on investment, considering the inexpensive rates of a policy. We don't use home or auto insurance regularly, but we still invest in them. Why wouldn't we do the same to protect our identities? Interested consumers wishing to take an extra step in protecting their credit will find some comfort and security in purchasing identity theft insurance.

Important amendments recently made to the Fair Credit Reporting Act

The Fair and Accurate Transactions Act of 2003 contains many amendments to the previous Fair Credit Reporting Act that help consumers resolve credit issues related to identity theft. In addition, this act introduces benefits that help them remain informed and ensure the accuracy of information contained in their credit reports.

Fraud alerts

To aid in the prevention of identity theft, upon a consumer's request (or that of any person acting on behalf of a consumer), a consumer-reporting agency must add a fraud alert to the consumer's credit file for a minimum of 90 days. After such a request is made, the receiving credit-reporting agency must notify other reporting agencies and provide the consumer with a free credit report within 72 business hours. The alert may be removed only upon the request of the consumer after he or she provides acceptable proof of identity. Consumers may request that an alert remain active for up to seven years.

The alert must be provided along with any credit scores produced using the credit report. If a seven-year alert is added, the credit-reporting agency must also remove the consumer from promotional marketing lists for a minimum of five years, unless otherwise instructed by the consumer.

Active duty alerts

Consumers who are in the military may request an active duty alert. This alert, added by a credit-reporting agency for a minimum of 12 months (unless otherwise instructed by a consumer) notifies creditors and other users that the prospective consumer does not authorize the establishment of credit, issuance of an additional card or increase in credit limit.

The only exception is if the creditor or user adopts reasonable procedures allowing it to believe it knows the identity of the requestor. The user may contact the subject of a credit report via telephone (if a phone number is provided with the alert) to verify the consumer's identity and confirm that the request is legitimate.

When a credit-reporting agency adds an active duty alert, it must also block a consumer's credit record from promotional marketing lists for two years, unless a consumer objects to such an action.

Truncation of Social Security numbers

Consumers who properly identify themselves may request that a consumer-reporting agency truncate the first five digits of their Social Security numbers from disclosure copies of credit reports. In addition, consumers advising the credit-reporting agencies that they may be victims of identity theft or fraud must be informed of their rights and advised by the credit-reporting agency of how to contact the Federal Trade Commission to determine what those rights are.

Lender responsibility related to identity theft and fraud

Any lender who establishes an unauthorized account or who allows an unauthorized transaction to occur must provide a copy of the application used to establish the account or a business transaction record of the unauthorized transaction (if a consumer makes the request in writing).

Before providing such information, a lender may require a victim (consumer) to provide proof of identity, a copy of a police report and a properly completed standard identity theft affidavit.

A lender may deny this type of request if it reasonably doubts the identity of the requestor believes the request is based on misrepresentation of facts.

Also, if the consumer requesting the information is able to obtain the a copy of the application or transaction history from the Internet, the lender is not obligated to send a hard copy. Instead, the lender can instruct the consumer to access his or her account online to obtain the information. This applies mainly to requests for transaction histories, as applications are not typically accessible online.

In addition, the Fair and Accurate Transactions Act prevents the sale and transference of debts resulting from identity theft or fraud. It prohibits debt collectors from making attempts to collect on such debts as well.

Access to credit information

The Fair and Accurate Transactions Act allows all consumers to receive one free credit report per year regardless of the state of residence. The report must be provided no later than 15 days after the request is received. Additionally, all consumers have the right to obtain credit scores from consumer-reporting agencies. The score must include the range of the scoring model used (lowest to highest), up to four key indicators (reason-codes) that adversely impacted the score generated and the date the score was produced. Under this law, a consumer-reporting agency may charge a fee (determined by the Federal Trade Commission) for producing a credit score with the aforementioned details.

Other amendments introduced by the Fair and Accurate Transactions Act of 2003 include the following:

- ◆ Consumers requesting to be removed from promotional marketing lists must be blocked for a minimum of five years, unless a consumer objects to such an action.

- ◆ Consumers may dispute information directly with furnishers. The furnisher must comply with the same guidelines as credit-reporting agencies with respect to the time frame for completing such an investigation. If the furnisher determines that the original information was incorrect, it must notify all relevant credit-reporting agencies to up-date their records. Dispute requests received from credit-repair businesses on behalf of consumers may not be honored.

◆ A reinvestigation by a credit-reporting agency that results in the update or deletion of an item on a consumer credit report must be shared with the furnisher. The credit-reporting agency is obligated to provide such notification.

◆ If a credit-reporting agency receives a request for a disclosure (that it honors) and the requestor's address differs substantially from the address the agency has on file for the consumer, the credit-reporting agency must notify the requestor of the address discrepancy.

The aforementioned are highlights of the Fair and Accurate Transactions Act of 2003. Please visit *www.ftc.gov* to find out about more important amendments made to the Fair Credit Reporting Act.

Chapter summary

The widespread uses of consumers' Social Security numbers and other personal data make it easier for their information to be compromised. Currently at the forefront of crime, it is probable that fraud and identity theft will continue growing, causing financial and emotional discomfort to many consumers.

The more we rely on computers and other automated processes that may have security flaws, the more likely it is for our private information to be in jeopardy. Avoiding common, inadvertent mistakes helps reduce chances of personal information from being exposed and fraud or identity theft from occurring.

I hate to sound like a broken record, but remaining informed of the content of one's credit report also helps in deterring risks associated with this terrible crime. If a consumer becomes a victim of fraud or identity theft, knowing one's rights, the parties to contact and the steps to follow will significantly curb frustrations and reduce completion time, stopping the culprit immediately in his or her tracks. Add value to your learning by completing the quiz on the following page. Good luck!

Chapter 10—Quiz

1. How might a consumer help prevent new accounts from being opened in his or her identity?

2. What was the leading form of fraud in 2002 according to the Identity Theft Clearinghouse?

3. What is the age range of the most targeted victims of ID theft?

4. What is the first action a consumer should take if he or she is a victim of ID theft?

5. What is the significance of filing a police report?

*** Bonus: What does identity theft insurance cover?

Chapter 10—Quiz Answers

1. A consumer may help prevent new accounts from being opened in his or her name by adding a fraud alert to his or her credit record.

2. The leading type of fraud resulting from identity theft in 2002 was credit card fraud.

3. The age range of the most targeted identity theft victims is 18–49.

4. A consumer should first contact the national credit-reporting agencies and have a fraud alert added to his or her file if he or she is a victim of identity theft.

5. A police report allows consumers to have fraudulent items removed from his or her credit record by a credit-reporting agency.

*** Bonus: ID theft insurance covers costs associated with correcting one's credit record due to fraudulent accounts.

Seeking Help From Credit Doctors

T here are some businesses that exist to help consumers remove accurate items from their credit records. These businesses might vary in structure and size, but most often contain key words in their advertisements such as "erase bad debt," "get a new credit report" or "get a clean credit report." Some may even pose as attorney offices that claim to specialize in the consumer credit-repair business. Credit doctors' meaning of credit repair is: "do everything we can do to get your derogatory information erased, whether it's true or not." In this chapter, we will review credit repair from the angle of credit doctors and discuss the risks associated with using their services.

Very often, credit doctors charge costly fees to act on behalf of consumers. They order copies of consumers' credit reports, contact credit-reporting agencies in writing or by telephone and dispute negative entries (whether legitimate or not) hoping that the reporting agency or creditor will drop the ball and allow the disputed item(s) to be deleted.

By "dropping the ball" I am referring to any of a number of possibile actions. The credit-reporting agency may have failed to re-verify the disputed item(s) within the specified time allotted by law or the furnisher of information may have failed to respond to a credit-reporting agency's request for verification within the time frame allowed. Other times, a furnisher of account information may not be able to verify data because it is old or obsolete. This may result in an item being removed from a consumer's credit record.

However, if the furnisher of information later verifies that the item previously deleted was correct, it may reinsert the item onto a consumer's credit record. Of course the amount of times an item was removed due to the inability of creditors to re-verify information is slim in comparison to their abilities to verify. The small percentage of times that items are permanently deleted from consumer credit records is partly responsible for the lukewarm success of these businesses.

These organizations are often referred to as "credit clinics" or "credit doctors." Aside from the aforementioned approaches, they utilize other techniques in an attempt to get adverse credit entries wiped off of consumer credit records. Credit doctors are quite often (or seem to be) well versed in the laws governing credit-reporting agencies and the re-verification process. More specifically, they are often familiar with the Fair Credit Reporting Act.

When employees from credit-doctor businesses contact credit-reporting agencies, they frequently quote specific sections of the Fair Credit Reporting Act and demand prompt action to correct a consumer's credit record. They are sometimes vague when conveying the nature of a consumer's dispute to credit-reporting agencies. This technique is used because it sometimes forces credit-reporting companies to make an educated guess about what a consumer may be disputing. It is an effort to make it difficult for credit-reporting agencies and creditors alike to be able to re-verify the authenticity of an account/debt.

For example, a credit doctor representing a client may contact a credit-reporting agency claiming that the Tri-State Auto account is "wrong," as opposed to stating the item should reflect a "zero balance."

This can be a very uncertain technique because it fails to specifically identify what is incorrect. Repetitive requests following this pattern could be viewed as frivolous and treated as such by credit-reporting companies.

There are guidelines outlined in the Fair Credit Reporting Act that protect credit-reporting agencies in consumer re-verification requests determined to be frivolous. If a credit-reporting agency determines in good faith that a request is frivolous, it is not obligated to reverify the information with the furnisher; in which case, a consumer will be notified in writing of such a decision.

Another technique that is growing in popularity among credit doctors is the practice of urging consumers to apply for a tax ID or employer ID number and use it to establish credit. This is by far the most preposterous, risky scheme of them all. Credit doctors may refer to this phenomenon in their advertisements as "building a brand new credit report."

Please be advised that it is illegal to receive an employer ID number and use it for the purposes of creating a brand new credit record. Further, if a consumer is successful in establishing a new credit report using an employer ID number, it does not automatically eradicate his or her original, legitimate credit record. In fact, it will create additional problems for a consumer.

First, credit-reporting agencies have relationships with the Social Security Administration and may possess other tools that help them determine the validity of a Social Security number. They may also be able to differentiate employer ID and tax ID numbers from Social Security numbers.

Secondly, creditors may be reluctant to extend credit to consumers who have established credit using both a Social Security and employer ID number. They may view this as an attempt to establish a fraudulent account and reject the application entirely. Consumers that buy into this ploy receive an employer ID number and use it as a Social Security number on credit applications.

If all else fails, credit doctors will continue to dispute the same items repeatedly, hoping for the desired result, which is ultimately to get them removed from a consumer's credit record.

Why do consumers use credit doctors?

Most consumers who solicit the assistance of credit doctors do so because they need help. The problem is that these consumers are often the ones who are unaware or entirely misinformed about the credit-reporting system and process of correcting their own credit records.

Further, there is another group of consumers who wish to avoid doing the work of contacting credit-reporting agencies, creditors, and so on, on their own. This sector prefers to pay another entity to get down in the trenches and do their dirty work, so to speak.

Lastly, there is a group of consumers that simply wants to "clean up" or "hide" derogatory entries on their credit reports. This group generally knows that most or all of the items on their credit records are correct, despite them being delinquent, but believe a credit doctor can erase them.

If you add to this the stories circulating about how difficult credit-reporting agencies can be, and consider how consumers often feel alienated by creditors and credit-reporting agencies, it becomes clear why they may resort to using credit doctors.

Think about it: How often do creditors and credit-reporting agencies advertise help to consumers regarding credit education? How often do credit-reporting agencies reach out to consumers at all, unless they wish to sell a product or service (especially one related to credit monitoring, credit scoring or identity protection)? Not often enough.

On the other hand, how often do creditors inundate consumers with unsolicited loan and credit card offers? Pretty often, I'd say. To the contrary, credit doctors tend to reach out to consumers more frequently, even if they have hidden agendas, and their sales pitches sound good to consumers. Hundreds of credit doctors can be located online; they advertise on radio and television; in most major metropolitan areas, they often have signs posted at exits off the expressways. Truly, they make themselves very accessible to consumers.

So, it makes sense that consumers look for credit doctors while avoiding debtors and credit-reporting agencies like a deadly disease. The nature of the relationship between consumers and creditors (and between consumers and credit-reporting agencies) is weak. When consumers do contact creditors and credit-reporting agencies, they often have their guards up and are defensive. Their past experiences dealing with these two entities, and sometimes a lack of understanding, influence such hostile behavior.

If credit doctors are so risky, why are they so popular and why do they continue to flourish? The answer is simple: many consumers are desperate for help with restoring their credit. However, when dealing with credit doctors, what consumers don't know can be detrimental to them. Furthermore, once most consumers pay a credit doctor, their chances of receiving a refund are slim, if not completely impossible. The prices charged by most credit doctors are outrageous. Depending upon the severity and amount of credit delinquencies, one could be asked to pay anywhere from a few hundred to several hundred dollars for services that cannot be guaranteed. It's a high price to pay for uncertainty.

Credit doctors often lure consumers by providing them with false expectations. Then they embellish and/or fabricate stories about what they claim credit-reporting agencies do to illegally penalize consumers. For example, they claim that credit-reporting agencies purposely alter important dates in an attempt to keep negative entries on credit reports longer.

I doubt that any credit-reporting company would intentionally risk violating federal law by taking such actions. The credit-reporting agencies do not stand to benefit by doing so, and acting in such a manner would only pose legal threats for them. Therefore, insinuating such a ploy is merely a scare tactic used by some credit doctors to further consumers' hatred and distrust of credit-reporting companies.

This argument does not indicate that important dates of credit entries never change, adversely impacting consumers; however, if such an action does occur, in the majority of cases, it is supplied by a furnisher or creditor to the credit-reporting agency. Generally speaking, furnishers and creditors are owed money; therefore, if any of the two parties (credit agencies or furnishers/creditors) has a motivation to alter dates, clearly it would be the latter. This could be viewed as a form of punishment to a consumer for not repaying a debt on time, or not at all.

This is one of many creative stories that credit doctors may employ to capture the attention of unsuspecting, vulnerable consumers who need help. I have approached a number of credit-doctor professionals during major events and financial seminars. It's both astounding and amusing to hear the plethora of misinformation they impart to unsuspecting consumers who are in need of credit assistance. They thrive on consumers who are in need of help—those who are desperate and wish to make a new beginning by creating a "clean" credit report.

While many consumers might be embarrassed to acknowledge they have been swindled out of money by a credit doctor, they should nonetheless report these incidents to the state attorney general's office and the Federal Trade Commission. In August of 2003, the Federal Trade Commission was instrumental in helping bring to justice one of the nation's most popular consumer credit "fix it" organizations: Nationwide Credit Repair.

Two companies, ICR Services and National Credit Education and Review sell their credit repair products under the title of National Credit Repair. These companies and their respective leadership teams were charged with violating federal law by claiming they could remove negative, albeit correct, information from consumers' credit records. Both parties claimed to accomplish this task by using a special computer disk and a top-secret process (also used, they claimed, by credit-reporting agencies to place derogatory entries on consumers' credit reports) to rid the reports of the information. All of these claims are false and were simply used as ploys to attract consumers' interest and money.

There is no such "top secret" process of reporting delinquencies to consumer credit records. The Federal Trade Commission also points out that no such disk exists, and the defendants did nothing more than write letters to the credit-reporting agencies disputing negative items on behalf of consumers (something consumers could have done for themselves). Further, the businesses were accused of charging consumers in advance for services that had not been rendered, which violates the Credit Repair Organization Act.

For their misleading, deceptive practices, National Credit Repair settled the Federal Trade Commission's complaints by forking out nearly 1.25 million dollars in restitution to consumers.

To report a complaint regarding an unfair experience with a credit doctor, contact the Federal Trade Commission online at *http://www.ftc.gov* or call 1-877-382-4357.

What should you do?

If you choose to solicit the help of a credit doctor, you should understand some critical facts. First there is absolutely nothing credit doctors can do for you that you cannot do for yourself. Yes, they may have more knowledge of credit laws and better understandings of the reverification process than you do. However, there are many reputable resources available that will provide the same information to you free of charge or at competitive costs, such as a certified consumer credit-counseling center. The only reason credit doctors appear to have expert knowledge is because it is their job to find loopholes in the process and take advantage of them when they do. And more than likely, you will be charged a fee for this knowldge, and a rather expensive one at that.

I once had a barber that paid over $1,000 to a credit doctor to correct an error on his credit report. In this case, there was an item on his credit report that truly did not belong to him, but belonged instead to his father (who had a similar name). Needless to say, this consumer was out the money, and the credit doctor did nothing to get the item expunged from his credit record.

I gave him only a fraction of the knowledge that I am imparting to you, and within a couple of weeks the derogatory item that did not belong to him was removed from his credit report. He was ecstatic that this process was over and that he was able to purchase the car he wanted; however, he was still livid that he lost a substantial amount of money trying to cut corners with a credit doctor.

Another thing to keep in mind, credit doctors cannot guarantee that items removed from your credit report will not be reinserted. The only way to know for certain that an item will be permanently removed from your credit record is to know the circumstances under which it was removed to begin with. In simple terms, this means that unless the item in question was truly erroneous or a creditor gave a credit-reporting agency specific instructions to remove the item from a consumer's credit record, it may be reinserted.

If you would really like to determine to what extent a credit doctor honors its work, ask them about reinsertions. Request that a provision be added into the agreement that allows you to receive a refund if any item removed as a result of it working on your behalf is reinserted by a creditor who subsequently verifies that the entry is correct. If the credit doctor is reluctant to agree to this request or totally objects, it's because it cannot guarantee its work. If their practices were ethical and sound, little doubt would linger about their ability to permanently rectify their clients' credit woes; in other words, they would guarantee their work.

Another concern to keep in mind, is that it is illegal in some states for credit doctors to charge money to consumers for providing credit assistance. To determine whether or not your state of residence has laws protecting consumers from the common iniquities of credit doctors or to report a problem you have experienced with one, contact your attorney general's office.

A final issue to keep in mind, credit doctors often dispute adverse entries that legitimately belong to consumers they represent. In the unlikely event that they are successful in getting such items removed, it will not prevent that creditor from continuing to pursue recovery of the debt. In other words, the original creditor or a contracted collection agency can still call and send threatening letters to you.

In addition, the creditor may file a civil judgment or garnishment in court, which could be picked up and appended to your credit record. Furthermore, just because a credit doctor is successful in having a legitimate item removed from one credit-reporting agency's database does not ensure that it will be successful in doing so with the other remaining credit-reporting agencies. Remember, credit-reporting companies are competitors; they do not (generally) share information with each other.

The verdict on credit doctors

Hopefully, I have made my points absolutely clear regarding credit doctors. If I have still failed to convince you of why you should avoid them and you still would like to seek their services, I encourage you to know your rights. The Credit Repair Organization Act lists guidelines that these organizations must adhere to in relation to consumers. Some of the most significant highlights are:

- ◆ Credit doctors cannot charge fees on any incomplete services they promised to render.

- ◆ Consumers may cancel a contract signed with a credit doctor within the three-day waiting period (beginning immediately following signature acknowledgement).

- ◆ Any contract signed with a credit doctor must specifically list the services to be rendered and must list the amount of time for completion of the work.

- ◆ Any contract signed with a credit doctor must list any guarantees offered.

Chapter summary

Choosing to do business with a credit doctor to restore your credit is risky and can be expensive. The biggest complaint consumers have against such businesses is paying for a service that is not delivered. It is senseless and unwise to pay for a service that is not guaranteed, expensive and that can be exercised by you at no charge.

In an effort to avoid paying a creditor, some consumers make the mistake of relying on credit doctors to rectify or undo past shortcomings. The money that consumers squander on credit doctors could go toward paying off debts they legitimately owe creditors. If applied in this manner, at least the action being taken is responsible and promises permanent resolution of an outstanding debt.

Do not pay credit doctors to do for you what you can do for yourself. Most of these companies prey on consumers' ignorance. For many consumers, the idea of having perfect credit or a clean slate is appealing enough to become lured by unrealistic claims of credit doctors. Credit doctors' most telling traits are their tenacity, aggression and swindling abilities, as opposed to their knowledge and integrity. If an offer or service sounds too good to be true, chances are it probably is.

Consumers opting to take a more practical approach to resolving past credit problems can do more for themselves than any credit doctor can. Refer to the chapter on disputing items on your credit report and bargaining with creditors for more detailed information.

One person's ignorance is another person's opportunity to dominate and control one's thinking. Allowing your judgment to become impaired by the thought of a quick and easy fix is a grave mistake that may have costly repercussions, including financial losses and personal setbacks.

Chapter 11—Quiz

1. What is a credit doctor?

2. Is it legal to establish a new credit report using a tax ID number?

3. Consumers can do for themselves what credit doctors charge money to do. (True/False)

4. Removal of items by credit doctors is always guaranteed. (True/False)

5. How many days does a consumer have to cancel a contract with a credit doctor?

*** Bonus: What is the biggest consumer complaint against credit doctors?

Chapter 11—Quiz Answers

1. A credit doctor is an agency or organization that relentlessly challenges legitimate credit entries in an attempt to have them removed from a consumer's credit record.

2. It is not legal to establish a new credit record using a tax ID number.

3. True

4. False

5. A consumer has three days to cancel a contract with a credit doctor.

*** Bonus: The biggest consumer complaint against credit doctors is that they pay for a service that repair companies do not deliver.

Credit Laws for All Purposes: Knowing Your Rights

Fair Credit Reporting Act

The Fair Credit Reporting Act is a federal body of law that was established to ensure accuracy and fairness of credit reporting with respect to consumers and the banking system. Its purpose is to assist in the uninterrupted functionality of the banking system by requiring the highest degree of accuracy in consumer credit reports and require consumer-reporting agencies to develop reasonable procedures for meeting the demands of commerce for consumer credit and other related fields with fairness to consumers.

The Fair Credit Reporting Act governs the behavior of creditors, the companies and credit-reporting agencies. It may be thought of as the credit bible. The Federal Trade Commission is the government agency who enforces the Fair Credit Reporting Act and helps protect consumers against wrongdoings of creditors and credit-reporting companies.

Every savvy consumer should be familiar with this body of law as its content details consumer rights and the responsibilities of creditors and credit-reporting agencies regarding credit reporting. The portions of the Fair Credit Reporting Act that are most important to consumers will be reviewed to equip you with the knowledge needed to defend yourselves from misconduct and unfair treatment.

Consumers have the right to dispute the accuracy of *any* item contained in their credit records. This right is outlined in section 611 of the Fair Credit Reporting Act. Some consumers may have been told that inquiries could not be reinvestigated. Contrary to popular belief, inquiries are susceptible to the same guidelines as any other piece of data appearing in a credit report. The Fair Credit Reporting Act does not make any distinctions or exceptions for inquiries. For this reason, any credit-reporting agency refusing to re-verify inquiries per a consumer's request is in direct violation of the Fair Credit Reporting Act and may be making itself an open target of litigation for noncompliance.

The reinvestigation process should not exceed 30 days from the date in which a credit-reporting agency receives the request from a consumer. However, the process may be extended for a maximum of 15 days if a credit-reporting agency receives additional, relevant information from a consumer.

Upon receiving a dispute request from a consumer, the credit-reporting agency has five business days to notify the creditor of the disputed information. Any relevant information, such as documents accompanying a dispute, must also be forwarded to the furnisher (of credit) in question. Relevant documents include letters and statements from creditors, copies of canceled checks, money orders, and so on, that a consumer can produce to support his or her claim.

Because such documents must be considered and acknowledged by credit-reporting agencies, it is always better to submit a request for re-verification in writing. It may be faster to request a reinvestigation via telephone or the Internet, but those channels do not provide as much room for holding credit-reporting agencies accountable as does the traditional paper and pen method.

A credit-reporting agency may cancel a reinvestigation request if it reasonably determines it to be irrelevant or frivolous. A sure way to have an investigation terminated is for a consumer to not specify the nature of his or her dispute. For this same reason, I previously warned of contacting credit-reporting agencies with vague requests. Consumers consulting credit doctors are probably more susceptible to this rule than the consumer who does not use those services. If a credit-reporting agency has reached the conclusion that a request is irrelevant or frivolous, it is allowed five business days to notify a consumer of such a cancelation.

Another example of a frivolous dispute that may result in the termination of a reinvestigation is receipt of repeat requests from consumers to reinvestigate items that have already been re-verified; more specifically, if a consumer fails to provide any additional, relevant information not previously submitted that might change the outcome of the reinvestigation. Any item(s) that cannot be verified or that is determined to be inaccurate or incomplete must be promptly expunged from a consumer's credit record or amended based upon the investigation results.

Reinsertion

An entry that is deleted due to any of the aforementioned reasons may be reinserted into a consumer's credit file if the furnisher of said information confirms that it is complete and correct. The credit-reporting agency is required to notify a consumer of such reinsertion within five business days after the item is appended to a credit record. Entries that are not certified as complete and correct by the furnisher may not be reinserted. The Fair Credit Reporting Act requires credit-reporting agencies to implement procedures to prevent the reappearance of deleted items that have not been confirmed as complete and accurate. Consumers may request that an updated, corrected credit report be sent to any company that previously received a copy of their credit report for employment purposes within the past two years. Updated copies may be sent to other companies that submitted inquires for other reasons within the past six to 12 months (depending upon the state of residence) from the date of correction.

Permissible Purposes: Section 604

Who can look at your credit report?

Section 604 of the Fair Credit Reporting Act stipulates the guidelines that allow credit-reporting agencies to grant viewing access to consumer credit reports. The frequency of times that a credit record has been viewed, commonly referred to as disclosure of a credit report, is recorded in the inquiry section. The inquiry section of a credit report displays a list of all individuals or firms who have been permitted viewing access to the content or requested some information about a consumer that was obtained from the credit report.

Access to a consumer's credit report may be granted under the following conditions:

(1) Court order. A credit-reporting agency that has received a court order or subpoena delivered regarding proceedings before a federal grand jury may permit access to a consumer credit record. A credit-reporting agency may receive an order from a court instructing it to block certain portions of a consumer's credit report due to fraud/identity theft. A court order may also be sent to a credit-reporting

agency in an attempt to locate a consumer, so as to issue a subpoena to appear in court.

(2) Consumer request. Receipt of a written request from a consumer to receive disclosure of his or her credit record must come directly from the person for whom the credit history belongs or from any party that the consumer has granted power of attorney. In short, this means that I cannot write a credit-reporting agency requesting a copy of your credit report and be permitted access, and vice versa. Further, if I do request your credit report, in order for that request to be honored, I must also supply legal evidence that I am authorized to receive that information.

(3) Potential lendors and collectors. A credit-reporting agency may grant viewing access to a person who intends to use the information to facilitate the extension of credit to a consumer or to collect on a consumer account. This refers to a consumer applying for credit with a lender, thereby giving the lender permission to access his or her credit record. It also allows debt-recovery companies to review or collect on a debt that is the responsibility of a consumer.

(4) Employment. Today it is very common for companies, especially those in the financial services industry, to require potential employees to permit access to their credit reports as a condition of employment. This may not be the only condition of employment, however. It may be used as one factor in selecting the best candidate for a position.

(5) Insurance. A credit-reporting agency may grant viewing access to a consumer credit report to a person/firm intending to use it for the purpose of underwriting insurance. Requests from consumers to receive auto, rental, life and homeowner's insurance may require that the carrier view their credit reports before extending an offer.

(6) Governmental licensing. Permission to view a consumer's credit report may be granted to a person who is attempting to determine the consumer's eligibility for a license or other similar governmental benefit. Review of a credit record is done to consider an applicant's current level of debt and his or her management of those responsibilities. This would apply to entrepreneurs seeking assistance in starting a small business, among others. Before such a license or governmental

benefit is extended to an applicant, law requires that the issuer determine the requester's eligibility.

(7) Valuation of credit or prepayment risks associated with an existing financial obligation. Viewing permission may be given to potential investors or servicers, or existing insurers, in order for them to determine whether an offer may be extended (and if limitations or deposits will be applied). This permissible purpose allows utility providers to access consumer credit reports and other related databases maintained by credit-reporting agencies to make credit decisions. The extent of how utility providers use consumer credit reports and other databases on payment behavior is discussed in Chapter 4.

(8) Legitimate business need. This is the permissible purpose that allows credit-reporting agencies to grant viewing access to people responding to other business transactions initiated by a consumer.

This permissible purpose also allows credit-reporting agencies to grant access to lenders who wish to review an existing account to make sure a consumer is still meeting the original terms of the agreement. If you have ever received a notice from your bank advising that your credit limit has been increased or decreased or that your account has been closed, it is the result of the bank accessing your credit report for review purposes. The bank is reviewing your credit report to determine how you are managing your credit overall. Indications that you are falling behind with other debts may warrant your bank taking adverse actions, such as closing your account or increasing your rates.

When a creditor raises a cardholder's interest rate after reviewing a bad credit report, it is said to be employing what's called a "universal default" clause. This clause, normally appearing in fine print on credit card applications and agreements, essentially states that a creditor can increase a cardholder's rate on an existing account if it discovers that the consumer has defaulted on another, unrelated debt. Indications that you have been managing your debts responsibly, on the other hand, may allow your financial institution to take positive actions, such as increasing your credit limit.

(9) Child support. Credit-reporting agencies may allow state or local child support agency administrators to view consumer credit

reports for the purpose of determining one's ability to pay child support and the amount to be paid. The maternity or paternity of the consumer in question must already be established under the relevant state laws, and the consumer must be notified (at the last known address) by the agency a minimum of 10 days prior to the credit report request. Any agency administering a state plan under section 604 of the Social Security Act may access a consumer's credit record to establish or modify a child support award.

Promotional inquiries

There are instances in which credit-reporting agencies may furnish consumer information for transactions not initiated by consumers. Most of these types of inquiries arrive to consumers in the form of promotional offers or preapproved credit applications. As long as a consumer has not elected to have his or her name and address excluded from preapproved marketing lists and the unsolicited transaction is a "firm" offer of credit or insurance, he or she may receive many unsolicited mailings from creditors.

What, then is considered a "firm" offer of credit or insurance? The Fair Credit Reporting Act defines a firm offer as any offer of credit or insurance that will be honored if the consumer meets the specific criteria used to select him or her for the initial offer. The determination that a consumer meets the specific criteria is based on information contained in his or her credit report. This means that a complete credit check will be performed after the preapproved application is completed and sent to the potential credit grantor.

The government's interpretation of the word "firm" may be a bit flawed and may require revisiting. Present consumers with the term "firm" and most will interpret the word as meaning "definite, unwavering and not subject to change." Most dictionaries describe the term "firm" in a similar fashion. The bottom line is, to use the word "firm" in a context indicating that an offer is pending or contingent on other factors is inappropriate and misleading.

Such practices certainly contribute to consumers' frustration and anger. In fact, some may believe that this type of aberration offers loopholes for creditors to send preapproved offers, but not honor these offers.

On the other hand, the Fair Credit Reporting Act's abnormal interpretation of "firm" may help creditors and insurance providers decrease the risk involved in extending credit. Creditors often receive lists of names and addresses from credit-reporting agencies. The lists are prepared based upon criteria specified by creditors. For example, a large credit card issuer may wish to target consumers who do not have much credit established, but no history of previous delinquencies on the thin credit files they do have.

With these factors in mind, credit-reporting agencies develop search criteria for their databases to manipulate and extract the names and addresses of such consumers. The problem is, consumers who may have met the unique criteria during the period when the list was originally compiled may have since experienced changes in their credit status. Therefore, by the time the preapproved offer has been received, they may no longer meet the specific criteria of the credit grantor.

To determine whether a consumer is still eligible for the offer and to receive a more complete picture of the consumer's credit standing, the creditor will access the consumer's credit report. It is in this manner that the Fair Credit Reporting Act's interpretation of "firm" aids credit grantors in limiting risk.

Getting your name off the lists

Consumers wishing to have their names and addresses excluded from preapproved marketing lists should contact the three national credit-reporting agencies in writing. Doing so will permanently block the consumer's name and address from the marketing lists these agencies compile. Making such a request by telephone usually allows only a two-year block to be implemented.

Consumers may also request that their telephone numbers be removed from telemarketing lists compiled by credit-reporting agencies. Credit-reporting agencies are not the only entities compiling lists and selling consumer names and addresses. Credit card companies, magazine distributors, charity organizations, retailers and other companies make lists of their customers, subscribers and members available to other businesses for a fee. In addition, there are list compilers who use various public and private resources to create databases for specific marketing audiences.

It all boils down to a recurring cycle of businesses selling and reselling consumer names and addresses to other businesses for a profit. Consumers wishing to have their names removed from mailing and telemarketing lists generated by businesses not affiliated with credit-reporting agencies should make their requests in writing to:

Direct Marketing Association
Telephone Preference Service
PO Box 9008
Farmingdale, NY 11735

Direct Marketing Association
Mail Preference Service
PO Box 9008
Farmingdale, NY 11735

Consumers should include their name, address and telephone number with their requests (include your Social Security number when contacting reporting agencies). Once such a request has made and received by a credit-reporting company, the agency has been five business days to comply. Conversely, a consumer may also cancel such a request and the block will be removed. This request should be submitted to a reporting agency in writing as well.

While the initial request to have credit-reporting agencies remove a consumer's name from marketing lists will be effective for two years, the credit-reporting agencies will subsequently send an election form allowing consumers to have their names permanently blocked.

Other access to consumers' credit information

In light of recent terrorist attacks, the federal government may receive other personal information as it relates to consumers. This type of disclosure is not provided for in section 604 (Permissible Purposes) of the Fair Credit Reporting Act; however, it has been specified in two amendments made after the September 11th tragedies.

The provisions are covered under the Strengthening America by Providing Appropriate Tools Required to Intercept and Obstruct Terrorism Act of 2001 (also know as the United States of America Patriot Act). These two amendments to the Fair Credit Reporting Act were put into effect October 26, 2001.

Under section 625 (Disclosure to the Federal Bureau of Investigation for Counterintelligence Purposes), a consumer-reporting agency will provide the Federal Bureau of Investigation with the names and addresses of all financial institutions that a designated consumer currently has an account or previously held an account with. Such a request must be made in writing and must include the signature of the Director of the Federal Bureau of Investigation or another employee designated by the Director. (If a designee has been selected, his or her position must not be lower than Deputy Assistant Director at the Federal Bureau of Investigation headquarters or a Special Agent having authority in a field office.)

The request must also state that the information is being sought in connection with an investigation aiming to protect against international terrorism or clandestine intelligence activities. Further, such an investigation of a United States citizen may not be carried out specifically on the basis of activities protected by the First Amendment to the United States Constitution. In other words, First Amendment rights may not be dishonored or violated by the investigation.

A consumer-reporting agency will also provide the Federal Bureau of Investigation with the designated consumer's name, address, former addresses, current and former employers and the consumer's credit report upon a similar written request received in writing.

A consumer-reporting agency that furnishes any of the aforementioned information to the Federal Bureau of Investigation is not authorized to make known to any party (other than associates or authorized agents of the agency itself) that the Federal Bureau of Investigation has either requested or been provided with the consumer report of a subject of such an investigation. This includes the consumer whose information was supplied.

In addition, a credit-reporting agency providing the data is prohibited from composing any subsequent credit report indicating that the Federal Bureau of Investigation has either requested or obtained any such personal consumer information. This means that consumers' personal information and credit records may be supplied to the Federal Bureau of Investigation without a reporting agency being legally obligated to disclose such a fact to the consumer. No type of inquiry will be appended to the consumer's credit record indicating such a request has been made or that such info has been provided.

The benefit to consumers is that this process has been designed to help curtail the likelihood of future terrorism in the United States. The benefit to credit-reporting agencies is more business. The Federal Bureau of Investigation pays them or reimburses them for costs they incur in collecting and reporting the information.

The Federal Bureau of Investigation may only share information obtained in this process with other federal agencies for the approval or conduct of foreign counterintelligence investigations or instances in which the information involves a person subject to the Uniform Code of Military Justice. Any division of the United States government violating the guidelines set forth in this portion of the Fair Credit Reporting Act is subject to pay compensatory damages to the affected consumer. In addition, if a court believes that circumstances leading to the violation may have been willful or intentional, the relevant agency or department must conduct an investigation to determine if disciplinary action is appropriate.

As long as credit-reporting agencies receive written certification of Federal Bureau of Investigation requests for consumer information, they are not liable for disclosing the data. This is considered a "good faith" attempt. This exception is to be observed by all levels of government.

Section 626 (Disclosures to Governmental Agencies for Counter-Terrorism Purposes) extends the same type of authority that has been given to the Federal Bureau of Investigation to other governmental agencies empowered to investigate intelligence or counterintelligence activities related to international terrorism. Credit-reporting agencies have to receive written certification from the agency making such a request. The leader of a federal agency (or an officer of a federal agency who is appointed by the president with Senate approval) must sign the certification.

Because these efforts are intended to assist in protecting national security, the fact that the government is allowed access to our financial records is one that many citizens can accept. However, governmental failure to comply with stipulations outlined will be an arduous fact to prove (if not virtually impossible due to the confidentiality subsections of the newest amendments). Consumers will not have the ability to determine (by reviewing their own credit report) if their personal information has been provided to either the Federal Bureau of Investigation or another governmental agency.

Traditionally, documentation of disclosure has been the most reliable, popular means by which consumers become aware of errors and unauthorized inquiries. Further, it maintains the ability to prove those injustices in court during litigation with credit-reporting agencies. Opponents believe privacy rights are severely compromised by the Patriot Act, and that citizen's civil liberties are being trampled on.

Equal Credit Opportunity Act

Equal rights when applying for credit

The Equal Credit Opportunity Act is a law that helps promote equal chances for consumers to receive credit. It prohibits credit grantors from considering factors such as race, national origin, sex, religion or marital status when deciding to offer credit to consumers. In addition, the law requires credit grantors to inform consumers of an approval or denial within 30 days of receiving a completed application. Further, the Equal Credit Opportunity Act is the law that requires creditors to provide *specific* reasons why an application was declined, if an applicant makes such a request within 60 days. Some examples of *valid* reasons are:

+ "Insufficient income."
+ "Credit limit to balance ratio is too high."
+ "Presence of a recent delinquency."

Examples of *unacceptable* reasons are:

+ "You did not meet our minimum criteria."
+ "Your score is not high enough."
+ "You did not qualify."

Lastly, if a consumer's application was approved but he or she did not receive exactly what was applied for (in terms of the credit limit, rates, and so on), he or she may request reasons for receiving the less favorable offer.

For example, imagine Jane applies for a credit card with 7.5% APR (annual percentage rate) and a $10,000 credit limit. However, she is only approved for a card with an APR of 12.9% and a credit limit of $5,000. Jane has the right to find out the reasons for the creditor's less attractive offer.

It follows that consumers also have the right to know the reason(s) why a creditor takes adverse action on an existing account. For example, if Janice receives a letter from her credit card company informing that the account has been closed, she must also be told the reason for such an action.

Any consumer believing that a creditor has violated his or her rights under the Equal Credit Opportunity Act is encouraged to make a complaint directly with the creditor. The Federal Trade Commission encourages the complainant to inform the creditor that he or she is familiar with the Equal Credit Opportunity Act. Additionally, the FTC also offers the following tips:

- Contact your state attorney general's office to determine if an equal credit opportunity state law has been violated.

- Report violations to the appropriate governmental agency.

- You may also be able to join others in the filing of a class action lawsuit or present a case in federal district court.

To obtain the name and address of the appropriate governmental authority for reporting violations of the Equal Credit Opportunity Act, log on to the following site on the World Wide Web: *www.ftc.gov/bcp/conline/pubs/credit/ecoa.html*.

Fair Credit Billing Act

The Fair Credit Billing Act's aim is to guard consumers from incorrect and unfair billing and credit card practices. This collective body of law represents the amendments made to the Truth In Lending Act. The highlights of the Fair Credit Billing Act will be discussed to provide a concise overview of the most significant portions that consumers should be aware of.

Billing errors

Consumers are not liable for portions of balances on statements containing billing errors provided they notify the creditor within 60 days of receiving the statement. However, they may only be exempted from the portion of the balance that contains the error; the remaining uncontested portion of the balance must be paid as normal. This rule usually applies to credit or charge cards in which a certain charge or purchase is being disputed.

For example, if Brandy makes a purchase using her ABC Bank Visa at Kohl's Department Store, but returns the merchandise the following day because she finds a better bargain at Sears, Kohl's should credit Brandy's credit card at the time the items are returned. If, upon receipt of her ABC Bank credit card statement, Brandy sees a charge for the returned purchase at Kohl's, she can dispute this charge by writing the credit card company within 60 days of receiving the statement. Further, she does not have to pay for that portion of her total balance.

Upon receiving a notice of dispute, a creditor must acknowledge receipt of a consumer's concern within 30 days. The creditor has an additional 60 days to research or investigate the dispute and either make any necessary corrections to the bill or send a written explanation to the consumer explaining why it believes the initial bill was correct. If the latter occurs, the consumer may require the creditor to provide copies of documentary evidence supporting its position.

Other types of billing errors covered under Fair Credit Billing Act are:

1) A fee or charge appearing on a statement that reflects an amount differing from the actual purchase the cardholder made.

2) A fee, charge or calculation on a statement for which a consumer requests documentary evidence or additional clarification.

3) A fee, charge or calculation on a statement for goods or services not accepted or not delivered in accordance with the agreement made at the time of the initial transaction.

4) A creditor's failure to reflect a payment made by a payee.

5) A computation or accounting error.

During the 90-day period that a creditor has to respond to and research a billing dispute, it may not restrict or close a consumer's account due to nonpayment of disputed charges. In addition, the creditor may not report adverse information to a credit-reporting agency regarding the payee's credit rating due to failure to pay a disputed amount. Similarly, it cannot report a delinquency to a reporting company regarding the contested amount until it has proven that the amount is correct and allowed the payee no less than 10 days to make payment.

If a creditor fails to comply with the guidelines, it relinquishes its right to collect on the disputed amount, including any related finance charges associated with the transaction. However, it is important to note that the amount in question must not exceed $50. If it exceeds $50, the creditor still possesses those rights.

Fair Debt Collection Practices Act

Dealing with collection agencies

The Fair Debt Collection Practices Act is an amendment to the Consumer Credit Protection Act. It was created to prevent abusive collection practices by third-party collectors and to endorse consistent actions by states so as to protect consumers' rights. In addition, it was designed to prevent any debt-recovery agencies that avoided abusive collection behavior from being penalized or placed at a competitive disadvantage to those companies that did engage in such practices.

Collectors attempting to locate an alleged debtor must comply with certain guidelines under the Fair Debt Collection Practices Act.

When communicating with people other than the alleged debtor, the collector must properly identify him or herself and advise the party contacted that this is an attempt to verify or correct the alleged debtors address. If asked, the collector must also provide the name of the company he or she represents.

The collector must not, however, divulge that the consumer being inquired about owes a debt, nor should this communication be made by postcard. In addition, if the person being contacted (who may have served as a reference on the original application) requests that the collector stop such contacts, the collector must oblige. An exception may be made if the collector reasonably believes the initial communication made resulted in an incorrect or incomplete response.

When communicating directly with an alleged debtor, a collector must also comply with certain guidelines. Section 604 of the Fair Debt Collection Practices Act lists the stipulations. Unless a consumer gives consent or a collector has received permission from a court with authority, the collector may not call a debtor before 8 a.m. and after 9 p.m. in the debtor's time zone.

A collector must also communicate with a consumer's attorney if he or she is representing the consumer with respect to the relevant debt and the collector is aware of the consumer's legal representation. The only exception that would allow a collector to revert back to communicating directly with the debtor is if his or her attorney fails to respond to the collector's communication or if the attorney advises the collector to communicate directly with the consumer.

A collector must not contact a debtor at his or her places of employment if the collector knows the employer does not permit such calls. In addition, collector communications with third parties is limited under normal attempts to recover a debt. Collectors may normally communicate with a consumer or his or her attorney, a consumer-reporting agency (where not prohibited by law), the original creditor or its attorney or the debt collector's attorney.

Finally, a consumer may advise a collector in writing of his or her refusal to pay a debt and advise the collector to end all further communication regarding the debt. This is known as a "cease communication" notice. After such a request is received, the only subsequent communication a collector may send to the debtor is:

- To advise that it is terminating any additional collection attempts.

- To advise that it may pursue alternate remedies to recover the debt.

- To advise that it intends to pursue a specific remedy to recover the debt.

The remedies referred to may be the filing of a claim (such as a judgment in court).

Collectors are prohibited from conduct that is abusive, harassing or oppressive when making collection attempts. Examples of misconduct and violation of this section include:

- The use of threats to inflict physical harm or damage to a person's reputation or property.

- The use of obscene language.

- The publication of a list of consumers who allegedly refuse to pay debts (except to consumer-reporting agencies).

- The advertisement of any debt for sale to coerce payment of the debt.

- Telephoning a consumer or conversing with a consumer repeatedly or continuously to annoy, abuse or harass.

- Telephoning a consumer and purposely avoiding disclosure of identity.

Sections 807, 808, and 812 of the Fair Debt Collection Practices Act detail false, misleading and unfair practices, and the use of deceptive forms respectively. These portions address ploys that some collectors have traditionally used in attempts to recover debts from payees. Consumers who are communicating with collectors regularly may find value in studying these three sections. They provide a specific list of collector actions and behavior that constitute violation of the law.

The Federal Trade Commission produces an annual report about compliance of the Fair Debt Collection Practices Act. Its report includes recommendations it believes will help improve compliance, enforcement and interpretation of the law. The report is based upon the type and number of consumer complaints received about abusive collectors.

In the report completed in April 2003 (concerning the previous year), the FTC reviewed consumer complaints. It received a total of 25,182 complaints from consumers regarding abusive collectors. More complaints were received regarding collectors than any other industry in 2002. The types of alleged abuse consumers reported ran the gamut from being threatened with violence to being called at work by collectors who were aware such calls were prohibited.

The Federal Trade Commission believes that this figure represents only a fraction of the true number of consumers who encountered abusive contact by third-party collectors. Additionally, the FTC has also stated that the number of consumer contacts made by third-party collectors is likely well into the millions.

There are a few reasons that may justify why the number of complaints is disproportionate to the number of contacts. First, many consumers are not aware that laws such as the Fair Debt Collection Practices Act exist to protect them from abusive collectors. In addition, a great many of consumers make complaints to governmental agencies other than the Federal Trade Commission. Many consumers complain to authorities at the offending collection company, and the majority of consumers do not complain at all.

Complaining to the Federal Trade Commission about abusive collectors is one of the best tools to bring about change in the industry. For example, in September 2002, The Associates and its parent company, Citigroup, agreed to pay $215 million in restitution to consumers, in part for violating the Fair Debt Collection Practices Act. In July of 2002, D.C. Credit Services, Inc., paid a civil penalty of $240,000 to settle charges that it violated the Fair Debt Collection Practices Act. Lastly, in April 2002, United Recovery Systems, Inc., paid $300,000 in civil penalties for violating the Fair Debt Collection Practices Act and the Fair Credit Reporting Act.

Consumers who believe they may have been victims of abuse from third-party collectors may file a complaint with the Federal Trade Commission online at *www.ftc.gov*, or via telephone at (877) 382-4357. A complaint number will be given to the consumer to confirm the recording of his or her complaint.

It is important to note that the Federal Trade Commission is not going to individually file a lawsuit or represent an individual consumer in court. If the Federal Trade Commission receives enough complaints about a company, however, it will conduct investigations to determine if the collector has violated the Fair Debt Collection Practices Act.

If a violation has been confirmed by the FTC's investigation, it will attempt to settle the issue with the offending company. If a settlement cannot be reached, the FTC may issue a formal complaint to the U.S. Department of Justice requesting a settlement for violations of the Fair Debt Collection Practices Act. If the collector still disagrees with the requested settlement or alleged charges, the Federal Trade Commission will request that the Department of Justice file a suit in federal court seeking injunctive relief and civil penalties.

Collectors must also comply with the Fair Credit Reporting Act. NCO Group, Inc., one of the largest debt-recovery businesses in the country, was charged with violating federal law when it reported incorrect information to credit-reporting agencies regarding consumers' accounts. The collection firm allegedly altered the original delinquency dates of collection accounts.

This date, also know as the date of last activity, determines how long the delinquent item remains on a consumer's credit report. By modifying the original delinquency dates of accounts, NCO caused adverse items to remain on credit reports in excess of the maximum seven-year period stipulated by the Fair Credit Reporting Act. Ultimately, the extension of such negative entries could adversely impact consumers' credit scores and result in denial of credit.

In May of 2004, NCO was ordered to pay $1.5 million dollars in civil penalties for violating federal law. In addition to the civil penalty, it was instructed to establish a system to evaluate complaints and help ensure that the information provided to credit-reporting agencies is accurate. Much like other violators of the Fair Credit Reporting Act, NCO also has to implement other tools to assist the FTC in measuring the company's future compliance with the Fair Credit Reporting Act.

The FTC continues to make progress in balancing consumer protection while minimizing the creation of laws thwarting collector's abilities to recover delinquent debts. In 2003, it made recommendations to Congress to add four amendments to the Fair Collection Practices Act in its efforts to strike such a balance. To find out more about the FTC's findings and proposals, please visit their Website at *www.ftc.gov*.

Chapter summary

The credit industry is convoluted and requires both regulation and strict adherence of laws in order to be impartial to consumers. The inception of many of these laws came into fruition because of complaints and mistreatment of consumers (in some capacity) by various parties. The evolution of the credit industry will continue to warrant the input and insight of state and federal governments.

As many of the members of the credit industry have historically failed to advise consumers of their rights, the FTC has been instrumental in providing some degree of comfort to consumers. The Federal Trade Commission is considered by many to be the vehicle that drives change related to fair treatment of consumers by the credit industry.

At the minimum, consumers should know that organizations involved in this industry are required to comply with laws, both state and federal. It would be an illusion to interact with collectors, creditors and reporting agencies and expect them to always uphold both your rights and their responsibilities.

Sometimes such failures are unintentional, but they occur often enough because they carry a low priority when compared with the goals of these businesses. For this reason, consumers have to be in control of their own education by becoming familiar with the relevant credit laws that impact them.

Chapter 12—Quiz

1. What agency enforces the Fair Credit Reporting Act?

2. Can consumers dispute inquiries?

3. How long does a credit-reporting agency have to notify a consumer that an entry has been reinserted?

4. What are Permissible Purposes?

5. Are promotional inquiries legal?

6. Under the Patriot Act, a consumer's personal information may be disclosed to a governmental agency without him or her having a right to be informed. (True/False)

7. What law allows consumers to know why they may have been denied credit?

8. What law allows consumers to challenge billing errors?

9. Under the Fair Debt Collection Practices Act, collectors may purposely avoid revealing their identity in order to recover a debt. (True/False)

Chapter 12—Quiz Answers

1. The Federal Trade Commission enforces the Fair Credit Reporting Act.

2. Consumers can dispute any part of their credit report.

3. A credit-reporting agency has five days to notify a consumer that an entry has been reinserted.

4. Permissible Purposes are reasons that allow a consumer's credit report to be viewed.

5. Promotional inquiries are legal.

6. True

7. The Equal Credit Opportunity Act allows consumers to know why they were denied credit.

8. The Fair Credit Billing Act allows consumers to challenge billing errors.

9. False

Complaints and Litigation Create Changes

I n June of 2002, in Spartanburg, South Carolina, three class action lawsuits were brought against the three national reporting agencies. It was alleged that the agencies reported certain consumers as having an account involved in bankruptcy filings.
However, the agencies failed to note that the bankruptcy claim filed
belonged to another party on the joint or shared debt.

*For example, Tom and Sarah shared responsibility of a Second
Bank credit card. Tom was laid off and eventually forced into bankruptcy. As a portion of liabilities, Tom claimed the outstanding credit
card debt in the bankruptcy.*

When Second Bank reports the account to the credit-reporting agencies, a statement is attached to the credit files of both Tom and Sarah reading, "account included in bankruptcy." If Second Bank does not clarify to the credit-reporting agency which of the cardholders actually filed for bankruptcy, the joint account Sarah shares with Tom reports the identical information on her credit record.

The problem is that the bankruptcy remark could cause Sarah to be denied credit because it gives the impression that she has become a higher financial risk. Since Sarah did not actually file bankruptcy, the account should appear on her credit report as either "account included in bankruptcy of another party" or "account is the responsibility of another party."

During trial preparations of the class action lawsuits, the defendants (the credit-reporting agencies), the legal team representing the plaintiffs and class members were ordered to participate in mediation proceedings. The primary purpose of mediation is to reduce risk and avoid a long, nasty trial for both parties. The risk was the defendants would succeed and the plaintiffs would receive nothing, primarily because these were the first class action cases brought against credit-reporting agencies in history. No precedent had been set to extrapolate the outcome of the current claims.

During the mediation in January 2003, negotiations were started to settle the pending cases before trial. The proposed settlement included the following:

- The defendants would alter their operating systems to eliminate and/or clarify bankruptcy references to joint account holders who did not file bankruptcy.

- The defendants would provide class members with free copies of their credit reports (credit files).

- After approval of the proposed settlement, any class member who proves a defendant violated the stipulations of settlement is entitled to receive payment of $500 from the defendant who failed to comply. Class members suffering financial damages of $75,000 or less may prosecute a claim through arbitration. Class members suffering financial damages exceeding $75,000 may exercise their right to sue in federal court.

◆ Class members relinquish the defendants from all liability claims made in the litigation based upon any credit report produced between April 20, 1998, and July 31, 2003.

On September 23, 2003, the settlement proposal (the same for all three cases) was reviewed by the court for fairness. The court concluded that proponents of the settlement had failed in proving why their requests or recommendations were necessary. However, the court conceded that the essence of the settlement proposal could be approved in the future if certain issues are addressed.

The court identified several flaws in the evidence brought forth by the proponents. First, the court believed the evidence was not sufficient in proving how altering the reporting system used by credit-reporting agencies would benefit class members and consumers in the future. They also exposed deficiencies in the terms listed in the stipulations of the settlement.

The court also addressed the concerns of those objecting to the stipulations of the settlement (those class members who believed the settlement was inadequate). The court believed the relief for prior damages was not an issue of debate. The objectors, however, maintained that the relief provided was inadequate to support their claims of prior damages.

In addition, the court disagreed with objectors who claimed the suggestions in the settlement intended to reduce future violations were inadequate. For example, one credit-reporting agency, Equifax, proposed a "fix" in which references pertaining to bankruptcies would remain, but be clarified by a statement reading: "bankruptcy belongs to (or is the responsibility of) another party." The court did not believe this proposed "fix" would violate the Fair Credit Reporting Act.

In closing, the court created a procedure that would allow the defendants and class counsel to work toward modification of the stipulations of settlement. The parties were ordered to provide objectors with the modifications by November 7, 2003.

To date, modified stipulations of settlement were filed, and the court has determined that the proposed fix was inadequate to resolve the issue. The court conducted a hearing on the fairness of the modified stipulations of settlement on January 12 and 13, 2004. The major credit-reporting agencies were ordered to discontinue making references to bankruptcies filed by third parties, whether qualified with additional wording or not. The credit-reporting agencies had to comply with this mandate by May 31, 2004.

As stated earlier, the significance of this case is that it was the first class action suit to be filed against the three major credit-reporting agencies, and it resulted in changes to the manner in which agencies report information about consumers' debt obligations.

In January 2000, the three consumer-reporting agencies agreed to pay $2.5 million to resolve allegations that they violated portions of the Fair Credit Reporting Act. The charges alleged the agencies failed to maintain toll-free telephone numbers during normal business hours, blocked millions of calls from consumers wishing to discuss possible mistakes in credit reports and forced some consumers to hold for lengthy periods of time. The allegations noted were brought into fruition by many consumers who conveyed their complaints to the Federal Trade Commission.

As a result of the complaints, the FTC began an investigation into the allegations. These complaints were filed by the United States Department of Justice on behalf of the Federal Trade Commission. Consequently, the three national consumer-reporting agencies are now required to meet certain performance standards proposed by the Federal Trade Commission.

Experian, Equifax and Trans Union must maintain toll-free telephone lines whereby personnel are available during normal business hours. Normal business hours are currently defined as 8 a.m. to 5 p.m. in each time zone. These lines are accessible to consumers who have obtained copies of credit reports directly from the three consumer-reporting agencies. If consumers obtain consumer credit reports from other sources that compile credit reports using access to the major credit-reporting agencies' databases, a toll-free telephone number granting access to live personnel may not always be available.

In addition, the consumer-reporting agencies are prohibited from blocking more than 10 percent of calls and must maintain a maximum average hold time of three minutes and 30 seconds. The consumer-reporting agencies are required to perform regular audits to ensure compliance of the proposed standards. As a follow-up to the regular audits required on each credit-reporting agency, one company, Equifax, was charged with violating the consent decree as little as one year after the first settlement.

The FTC alleged that the reporting agency did not have adequate staff available to answer consumer calls in 2001. As a result, the hold time requirements were not met and the number of telephone calls blocked by Equifax exceeded 10 percent. As the agency again failed to meet performance standards, in July 2003, it agreed to pay $250,000 to settle charges. This is more evidence supporting the progress being made by the Federal Trade Commission to help ensure fairness to consumers in the credit-reporting process.

Chapter summary

All of the aforementioned cases or settlements demonstrate the strength of the collective consumer voice. I caution consumers to make sure their requests are ethical and needed in order to bring about improvements, rather than exercising taking advantage of loopholes in the existing system. I say this because the credit industry is filled with corporations that have lots of money to defend and honor their causes.

Collectively, the credit industry's ability to mobilize and influence the outcomes of many laws and decisions is greater due to their power; remember, money is power. Many of them have lobbyists vying for or opposing pending legislation.

While consumers have been able to make significant gains, they must always be aware of the position and strategy of their detractors. Consumers may not possess the same financial and political clout as big businesses, but if carefully organized and prepared, they can obviously create change.

Chapter 13—Quiz

1. Credit-reporting agencies may only block _____ percent of consumer calls they receive.

2. A credit-reporting agency call center's average hold time for consumers should be a maximum of _____ .

3. The hours that credit-reporting agencies must offer live telephone assistance are 9 a.m. to 7 p.m. Eastern Standard Time. (True/False)

4. What resulted in a change in reporting practices of credit-reporting agencies?

Chapter 13—Quiz Answers

1. Credit-reporting agencies may only block 10 percent of consumer calls they receive.

2. A credit-reporting agency's call center's average hold time for consumers should be a maximum of three minutes and 30 seconds.

3. False

4. A class action lawsuit regarding bankruptcies affecting joint accounts.

Helpful Information

The objective of this chapter is to focus on other aspects that affect consumer credit. Most, if not all, are important topics frequently omitted from consumer credit guides or quietly considered with little depth or discussion. By reading this chapter you will understand how uniformity is maintained among the credit agencies. You will also learn how check verification companies operate and what new check clearance laws are in the works. I will also explain the hype and truth about the fourth credit-reporting agency, and you will learn about the new types of collection companies. Additionally, Canadian consumers will learn how to go about establishing credit in the United States.

Consumer Data Industry Association

The Consumer Data Industry Association is an organization representing companies involved in the business of consumer information. It supports companies who provide risk-management and fraud-prevention solutions, credit and mortgage reports, tenant and employment screenings, check verification services and collection services.

The Consumer Data Industry Association is mostly known for its role as spokesperson for the national credit-reporting agencies in the media. It also represents the credit-reporting industry before state and federal legislators as well.

Additionally, the Consumer Data Industry Association has been instrumental in creating automated reporting and consumer dispute resolution standards for the credit-reporting agencies.The most notable development in automated consumer dispute verification and automated data updating is the development of E-Oscar (Online Solution for Complete and Accurate Reporting). This is a system that has brought about many benefits related to helping consumer-reporting agencies resolve consumer disputes promptly and accurately. It has also aided furnishers of credit in ensuring updates to records on consumer credit reports are timely and correct.

Overall, the Consumer Data Industry Association helps to maintain uniformity among the three national consumer-reporting agencies in regards to the most important aspects of credit reporting, dispute resolution and credit file updating.

The Consumer Data Industry Association has also played a significant role in making the process of adding consumer fraud alerts easier. Now, consumers may have fraud alerts added to the credit records of all three national credit-reporting agencies by making a single telephone call to one of the "big three" companies. The agency who receives the initial call from a consumer requesting a fraud alert due to identity theft will electronically advise the other two reporting companies of the crime, and the fraud alert should be added within 24 hours. In addition, the consumer's request for a copy of his or her credit report will be processed within 72 business hours.

If the consumer files a police report concerning the incident, the three national credit-reporting agencies will immediately remove fraudulent data without conducting a normal 30-day reinvestigation of the fraudulent accounts.

Further, 90 days after the fraud reinvestigation, the agencies will follow up with consumers by sending a free credit report to them. This allows consumers to review their credit records to ensure that no subsequent fraudulent debts have surfaced and been reported in their names. Prior to this initiative, consumers had to place a separate call to each of the three national credit-reporting agencies to have a fraud alert added to their credit records.

The Consumer Data Industry Association is a trade association that only offers membership to businesses operating in the consumer infor- mation field. The majority of its members share a common factor— that is, the laws of the Fair Credit Reporting Act regulate them all. Entities excluded from membership include commercial banks, retail stores, bank- card issuers, credit unions, mortgage brokers, real estate agencies and savings and loan institutions.

Check verification companies

How many consumers have ever written a personal check only to be informed their check has been declined. Next to being denied credit, this is probably the most humiliating and embarrassing infomation to receive from a merchant. I would like to share a story with you detailing my experience with this anger-provoking and flawed process.

However, before I begin it is necessary to note that credit-reporting agencies may or may not be affiliated with check verification companies. For example, one check verification company, Certegy, is affiliated with major credit-reporting agency Equifax. In fact, a few years ago, Certegy was known as Equifax Check Services. Some of the names of other major players in the check verification field are Scan and Telecheck.

Check verification companies exist to help merchants reduce risks associated with accepting checks as a form of payment from consumers. Guidelines are created that determine whether or not a consumer's check will be approved or rejected. The participating merchant and the check verification company most likely create these criteria. If the criteria are met, a consumer's check will be accepted and approved. On the other hand, if the established criteria are not met, the consumer's check will be declined, leaving him or her with the burden of producing an alternate form of payment for services rendered.

This entire process seems to parallel the traditional scoring system that is used in credit application procedures. The check verification process undoubtedly incorporates some of the same unique features present in scoring models, such as reason-codes for declination.

Getting back to my own experience with the check verification process, about three years ago I took my vehicle to an auto repair company to receive a scheduled major tune-up. Depending upon the make of the automobile, the cost for this service is typically between $500 and $1000. In addition to the major tune-up, I also purchased four brand-new tires. At any rate, the total amount due to the merchant was around $1,200.

Like many consumers, I do not walk around with that amount of cash in my wallet. In addition, I did not want to charge the purchase to a credit card and risk incurring finance charges for carrying over a balance (yes, even I become tempted by the notion of making smaller payments). So, I decided to pay by check. I will never forget presenting the check along with my identification only to be informed that my check "didn't go through."

It hit me in the face like a ton of bricks! I had never written a check in the past that bounced, and the funds were in my checking account. This was impossible! "How could it be?" I wondered and demanded an explanation from the service center's employee immediately.

The employee could only say, "I'm not sure, it just says: the check presented was declined for reason-code two." After probing her for additional information regarding this reason-code and inquiring about its exact meaning, I was given the name and telephone number of the check verification company (Certegy) who declined my check and was instructed to call them directly to receive more information. In the meantime, I had to charge the total amount due on my credit card.

This was a huge inconvenience to me and I was completely confused. I kept thinking, "How could they [Certegy] make a decision to decline my check without even providing a valid reason, and why couldn't the merchant use better judgment and override this premature, inconclusive decision?" After all, I had worked in the credit industry and gained exposure to many processes that befuddled most consumers at the very least.

I imagine I felt the same way a consumer feels when he or she is denied credit and given no valid explanation as to how and why that decision was derived. However, I was determined to unravel the truth and understand this unique check verification process. I know this might sound rather pretentious, but I had not been denied credit in a several years. So, in my mind, being declined was unacceptable.

I called Certegy to receive an explanation. As is often the case in contacting credit-reporting agencies, I encountered telephone automation presenting several options and prompts, none of which offered a live customer service representative. I was forced to input information into their system and wait several days to receive (in writing) reasons surrounding the declination of my check.

When the letter finally arrived, it advised that my check "fell outside our approval guidelines and we do not have enough positive information to override the check decline." Of course I thought this a bunch of fluff that didn't even address the obvious question as to why I was denied the ability to write a check.

Fortunately, much like consumer credit reports, a toll-free telephone number was provided on the letter. It wasn't until I called and probed intensely that I was given, in simple and concise terms, the true reason that my check was declined. My check was rejected because Certegy had no check-writing information about me in their database. This is the same as a consumer being denied credit because he or she does not already have some credit established. For merchants, making the decision to accept or reject a check is driven by the risk factor.

After I had absorbed everything that had taken place, I began to realize that this process was designed to help merchants reduce risks, much like scoring models were created primarily to help creditors reduce risks and identify the best candidates for credit. Although I did not find much comfort in conceding to this fact, I had a better understanding of the entire check verification process.

Consequently, I was sent a Gold Application from Certegy. This gold membership would apparently allow them to establish me in their system as a check writer and supposedly prevent situations like the one I encountered from occurring in the future.

The Gold application requested the following information: name, address, telephone number, state that issued driver's license and driver's license number, date of birth, employer's name and length of time employed and complete checking account information (including the opening date, account number, average daily balance and whether it includes overdraft protection). All of this information is personal. I refused to divulge that information to a company that stands to gain a profit off me and reject my checks simultaneously.

I was not interested in obtaining such membership, and I remain so. My position is that if a merchant is simple enough to allow a check verification company to decline my check based upon a reason it did not even understand, I have no desire or need to conduct business with it. I later discovered that merchants have free will to override the decisions made by check verification companies.

If more merchants begin using check verification companies, a bad precedent will be set. Consumers will literally have to apply for check-writing privileges in order for their checks to be approved. Merchants would be wise to carefully consider the pros and cons of using check verification systems.

Some retailers have discontinued use of check verification systems due to the potential loss of sales. Shoppers become irritated that their checks may be rejected based upon something as trivial as a change of address or different driver's license number (yes, a check may be declined or one may encounter hassles by one of these systems because a consumer moves and the check verification company does not have his or her new address and telephone number or their driver's license number in their database).

For consumers seeking gold status through Certegy, once approved, they are almost guaranteed hassle-free check writing in the future. In this process, Certegy is certifying check-writing privileges and screening out candidates for merchants. However, membership allows Certegy to charge a service fee of $25 or more as regulated by law for any subsequent dishonored check that a consumer may present.

Considering all the facts, I cannot determine the worthwhile benefit to consumers, other than the comfort of hassle-free check writing. The trend here is that consumers will have to apply for acceptance of their checks even after establishing a checking account with a bank or other financial institution.

Canadian consumers and how to establish credit

Canadians moving to the United States and seeking to establish credit have the ability to do so with greater ease than consumers moving to the United States from other parts of the world. In the credit industry, there is a system referred to as the North American Link. This allows creditors in the United States and Canada to exchange some information about credit established in Canada, and vice versa. Without such a system in place, consumers run the risk of starting over with establishing credit from scratch, which may include being denied credit.

For consumers moving between the United States and Canada, it behooves them to inquire about this shared information link. If the creditor that a consumer is seeking to do business with is a member of the North American Link, it may help alleviate normal burdens consumers face while establishing credit in another country.

Canadian consumers are assigned social insurance numbers in the same manner that American consumers are assigned Social Security numbers. They should avoid at all costs using their social insurance numbers as a Social Security number to establish credit in the United States. The Canadian social insurance number has the same amount of digits as an American Social Security number.

Because of the similarities in length and the inability of consumer-reporting agency databases to distinguish between the two, credit records may become entwined. For example, a social insurance number may convert or equate to a real Social Security number assigned by the United States government to an unknown consumer. If the Canadian citizen is approved for credit, his or her information will possibly be crossed with that of the American consumer who has been assigned a similar Social Security number. This could create a mess for both parties.

Consumers from Canada seeking to establish credit in the United States should follow normal procedures for obtaining a Social Security number and then apply for credit after receiving one. Another alternative is for consumers spending ample amount of time in each country to own widely accepted credit cards such as Visa and MasterCard.

The fourth credit-reporting agency

There is increasing discussion among consumers about the existence of a fourth consumer-reporting agency called Innovis Consumer Assistance. Based in Columbus, Ohio, Innovis is at best a small, fledging newcomer in the credit-reporting industry.

Most creditors do not submit consumer account information to Innovis, and this results in the company having very limited data and influence. The less information Innovis reports, the less useful and attractive it is to credit grantors.

A consumer report containing little data is not as reliable in helping credit grantors make decisions to extend or decline applications for credit as one with a list of accounts indicating previous performance.

Therefore, at the present time, most creditors continue to utilize the three nationally recognized consumer-reporting agencies (Equifax, Experian and Trans Union).

Innovis claims to be currently gathering data from creditors and other sources so as to eventually compete with the three major credit-reporting companies. Unfortunately, many creditors are not contributing to Innovis's database. Innovis does not currently have the ability to prepare credit scores for consumers or credit grantors. However, consumers may still request copies of their credit records from this agency.

Recently, I requested a consumer credit report from Innovis out of curiosity. It only listed two of several accounts I currently hold or have held in the past, and no inquiries. The report was accompanied by a research request form in the event a consumer disagrees with information on the file. The credit report contained the same basic information that the others offer, and had no noteworthy differences worth mentioning. Consumers may contact Innovis Consumer Assistance at the following address in order to request a copy of their credit records:

Innovis Consumer Assistance
PO Box 134
Columbus OH 43216-1534

Check-clearing for the 21st century—Check 21

All consumers should be aware of a new federal law regarding checks. Effective October 28, 2004, banks are allowed to exchange checks electronically. This process allows images of checks to substitute for physical copies. Commonly referred to as Check 21, the federal law recognizes a check image as the legal reciprocal of a paper copy. Check 21 was spurred primarily by the virtual shutdown of the conventional system during the aftermath of the September 11th terrorist attacks.

The significance of Check 21 is that it allows checks to clear faster, especially large checks that are from other states. Early speculation predicts that out-of-state checks may eventually clear within 24 hours, competing fiercely with the clearance time of local checks. Consumers who practice a technique called "floating" may be at most risk as a result of Check 21 going into effect. "Floating" is defined or understood as writing checks on accounts that have insufficient funds, hoping that appropriate funds will be available by the time the check clears.

In the past, consumers could estimate the length of time it would take for a check to clear, especially for merchants or creditors who are paid regularly by check, such as landlords. But thanks to Check 21, their check-clearance predictions will likely be skewed. Consequently, consumers who continue floating will realize an increase in the number of returned checks.

Obviously, a history of returned checks severely impacts consumers. First, the recipient of a returned check is going to assess a returned-check fee and additionally be charged a late-payment fee. Then, the merchant may refuse to accept future check payments from the consumer and require him or her to use an alternative form of payment such as a credit card, debit card or money order. Further, the consumer's bank is going to charge an insufficient-fund fee. If that's not enough punishment, check verification companies such as Telecheck, Scan and Certegy may receive notification of the occurrence, affecting one's ability to write checks to many other merchants. Consider yourself warned of the perils floating can bring.

Early speculation has concluded that all banks will have check-imaging transfer systems installed and in utilization by 2008. The conversion to electronic check imaging will be a gradual one over the next four years or so. This will afford consumers time to adjust to the new process and banks the ability to spread out costs associated with acquiring equipment and implementation systems required by the new process. Banks are expected to reduce normal operating expenses associated with shipping and processing paper checks across the country. They are also expected to begin charging or increasing fees to customers opting to receive their checks back.

Consumers should anticipate receiving notices from their banks regarding how the inception of Check 21 will affect them. Consumer advocates' advice is for everyone to expect their checks to clear faster; hopefully, this assumption will encourage consumers to write and submit only checks that they have the funds to cover. Doing so will reduce risks and repercussions of bad check writing and preserve the privileges created by the convenience of checks.

Beware of the new generation of collectors

A new breed of collectors who purchase the bad debts of various financial institutions is on the rise. As a way of offsetting losses from nonpaying consumers, retailers, utility companies, credit card providers and lenders alike are beginning to sell their bad debts.

Traditionally, these institutions consult third-party collectors to launch aggressive campaigns on consumers to recover unpaid debts. If the collection agency is successful, it receives a percentage of the amount recovered. On the other hand, if the collection agency is not successful after a certain period of time, the unpaid debt is returned to the client (original creditor) as "uncollectible."

This sector of the collection industry is growing exponentially. The amount of bad debts purchased in 2003 rose to 57.3 billion dollars, up from 660 million dollars just 10 years before. In some part, I attribute the growth and success of this business to the lack of understanding and education of many consumers.

The new wave of collectors differ from traditional ones in a number of ways. First, they purchase bad debts outright from creditors for a fraction of the initial amount owed by a consumer. Buying the debt allows the collector to retain 100 percent of profits reaped if the debt is recovered. For a lender, selling the bad debt allows it to recover a portion of the money it was unlikely to obtain from a consumer.

These ingenious collectors have reputations of using small claims and municipal courts to file suits against consumers in efforts to recover debts. Threatened and dismayed by the idea of litigation, the overwhelming majority of consumers do not show up to court to find out more information about the debt or to dispute the validity of it. Because they don't, many times the collector is allowed to swiftly obtain a judgment and pursue more promising measures for procuring payments, including garnishment of a consumer's wages or seizure of one's assets. At this point, the collectors have usually attached additional fees (such as interest and court costs) that sharply augment the original amount of the debt.

What consumers don't realize is that the ability of the collector to prove the validity of such debt is severely hampered by poor record-keeping. Sometimes a bad debt goes from a client (original creditor) to a conventional third-party collector, and then back to the original client again. Finally, the debt is sold to one of the nontraditional collectors.

During these ownership transitions, important information about the debt is often lost. I'm referring to information such as the original delinquency date or even appropriate and acceptable evidence linking a consumer to a debt (such as the original credit application). Some attorneys representing consumers have challenged these collectors in court and been successful in having the cases either dismissed or settled due to a lack of evidence or distortion of facts.

Portfolio Recovery, Asset Acceptance Management and Anderson Financial Network are three examples of companies that may purchase bad debts and attempt to return a profit by recovering monies due from consumers.

From my experience working for a major credit-reporting agency, I'm inclined to argue that these types of companies typically have poor documentation of consumer debts. In fact, the majority of times consumers contest the accuracy of such entries on their credit records, the collector either does not respond to the credit-reporting agency's investigation request, responds with instructions for the agency to remove the debt because certain key data cannot be verified or it provides illogical information about the account that forces the reporting agency to delete it anyway.

The most common example of how a collector provides illogical information is when the collector supplies an opened date for an account that occurs (in time) after the date of last activity (or the original delinquency date). For example, let's say an account was charged off in November of 2002, but the collector submits an opened date of May 2004, to the credit-reporting agency.

Logically, the opened date must always precede the date of last activity; otherwise, the account would have become delinquent before it ever existed. Some collectors mistakenly submit the date they purchased the debt from a creditor as the date the account was opened, which is inaccurate. The correct opened date is the one on file from the original creditor. This supports the observation made earlier regarding the poor bookkeeping habits of many collectors.

Some argue that inadvertently or intentionally altering important dates is a collector's attempt to force the account to remain on a consumer's credit record longer than the law stipulates. This is possible. Consumers uncertain about the accuracy, completeness or validity of these types of debt are encouraged to challenge them in court.

Chapter summary

There are various other facets affecting consumer credit that are often omitted from credit and financial guides. Check verification companies and the other businesses discussed are just a fraction of the available services with ties to the credit industry.

Consumers would do best to read a variety of periodicals and other material related to personal finance. Doing so will keep them on the cutting edge of developing trends occurring in the financial and credit industries that may or may not be derivatives expressly introduced by credit-reporting agencies or its affiliates.

Chapter 14—Quiz

1. Can anyone join the Consumer Data Industry Association?

2. What standards have been instituted by the Consumer Data Industry Association to create uniformity in the credit-reporting industry?

3. Name one check verification company?

4. Could a consumer's check be declined if he or she has no history of writing a check that bounced?

5. What common practice of consumers may be affected by Check 21?

6. How do new collection agencies primarily differ from traditional ones?

*** Bonus: Innovis Consumer Assistance is a big competitor to Experian. (True/False)

Chapter 14—Quiz Answers

1. Membership to the Consumer Data Industry Association is limited to organizations that are engaged in the consumer information industry and regulated by the Fair Credit Reporting Act.

2. The Consumer Data Industry Association has standardized consumer dispute verification and fraud procedures among the three national credit-reporting agencies.

3. Scan, Telecheck, and Certegy are names of three check verification companies.

4. A consumer's check may be declined even if he or she has no history of writing a check that bounced.

5. Check 21 could affect floating.

6. New collectors purchase bad debts from creditors and traditional collections do not.

*** Bonus: False.

Afterword

Take control of your credit

If after reading this book you are still blaming credit-reporting agencies, creditors, your ex-spouses, collectors or the reporting system for your credit woes, you may not have received the underlying message of this material. If so, you may need to read it again from front to back.

I am not arguing that there are no uncontrollable factors that arise, inhibiting consumers from fulfilling their credit or debt obligations. I understand that divorce or the receipt of a pink slip from work can have devastating impacts on one's ability to repay creditors. However, you must have a contingency plan in place to help offset or ameliorate the severity of such life-changing occurrences.

Do not overextend yourself in debt through excessive loans and credit cards. Stop following every move the Jones's make, and, above all, stop relying so heavily on credit! A person earning $35,000 a year, with little or no debt, is more financially secure than a millionaire who is indebted to several people. Economically successful people may use credit, but do not depend on it.

I understand that many consumers don't want to give up credit, and that others are just not disciplined enough to let it go. However, real-life experiences have taught me the same lessons they've taught you. If you use credit, it must be used responsibly. I commend all of those that have the willpower and discipline to carry a credit card in their purse or wallet without making a capricious purchase. For the remainder and overwhelming majority of us, we have to learn self-control and discipline.

How, you ask? Only apply for credit that is needed. The phrase "this is just for emergency purposes" does not justify you having multiple credit cards, nor does it justify carrying balances (high or low) on each of them. If you have the credit cards, you will be tempted to use them. I recommend that consumers have no more than two active credit cards.

Submitting department store charge card applications to receive a small discount on purchases is just a ploy to get consumers to open accounts. The department stores know that once an account is established, it will not remain unused. Since most department stores have extremely high rates, it does not benefit you to use them frequently unless you can pay the entire balance upon receipt of the statement.

Additionally, protect your credit by shopping for the most competitive rates and being cautious about entering into contracts with another person, especially if the other party is repaying the debt that your established, good credit helped him or her acquire. Remember that the manner in which he or she handles the debt will also affect your credit rating. Try to make banks and creditors match or surpass offers of other lenders. Employee credit unions are a great place to begin when shopping for credit. Historically, these institutions have the best rates in the industry.

Exercise sound judgment. Remember, if something sounds too good to be true, chances are it probably is untrue. Read everything that is written and listen to everything you're told. And then read between the lines and have any unclear information explained. For some reason, most consumers hate reading. Some of us can't understand the lofty terminology that creditors use and are afraid to ask for explanations.

Another example of using good judgment is notifying a creditor ahead of time if you will not be able to make a payment on the due date. Negotiating better rates with lenders is also practicing good judgment. So is considering all the facts and elements of a situation (positive and negative) that may affect your reaching your financial goals. Once those elements have been evaluated, you must be empowered to make a decision through right action.

What is exercising "right action"? It is paying on a debt instead of not paying it or, worse, completely ignoring your credit obligations. It is actively challenging the rules and standards of the credit industry designed to keep consumers bewildered and at a competitive disadvantage. Exercising right action is behaving in a manner that employs precepts that you know are fair and unbiased. Practicing right action is not trying to erase debts that are legitimately yours by consulting a credit doctor, but addressing them head-on and taking control of negotiations to repay them. Right action is challenging your creditors to report correct information promptly to credit-reporting agencies. You have a voice and now you have the knowledge. Be confident and challenge the status quo.

In order to remain on the cutting edge of the credit industry, you must constantly seek additional training. Your education does not stop after reading this book or any other books marketed on this subject. Always seek additional information. Read, read and read some more.

In selecting your sources of information, determine if the provider is reliable based on his or her credentials. Ask questions such as, "Is this person qualified to speak on this subject, and, if so, what are his or her qualifications" and "How much of this material contradicts other respected information published about this subject?" You must not be fooled into thinking a person is an expert based solely on his or her education level or because of their career position. Dig deeper than the obvious and do not be afraid to challenge one's credentials.

Similarly, visit the Websites of the major credit-reporting agencies, the Federal Trade Commission and consumer protection organizations such as A Call for Action. Often, you will find very helpful data on these Websites, as well as links to other information sources.

Remaining informed will help you decipher fact from fiction, and your education will allow you to act confidently in your dealings with creditors and credit-reporting agencies. Further, it will allow you to challenge everything you are unsure about or disagree with. The cliché "knowledge is power" is very applicable when considering personal credit and finances. I implore you to apply your knowledge actively, at every opportunity presented and, most of all, to not give up a fight for what you know is right.

Remember, also, if you are not receiving prompt and adequate responses to your credit questions, escalate, escalate and escalate some more! Trust me when I tell you that executives have more pressing concerns to address than speaking to an angry consumer.

This is not to suggest that consumers' concerns are not important, but most managers at this level are so detached from the daily operational processes and are incapable of offering the type of assistance needed that he or she will gladly delegate the job to someone else. In doing so, they will likely convey a clear message that a customer's escalation to that level is not unacceptable and is a result of customer service personnel failing at their jobs. It will also be communicated that the consumer's needs must be resolved immediately.

Unfortunately, because of corporate bureaucracy, some executives are oblivious to counterproductive, ineffective processes until a resolute consumer reaches him or her and exposes the truth by escalating. If this is the route that must be traveled in order to influence change, I admonish you to pack your suitcase to capacity with knowledge and then embark upon this journey. From my own personal experience, I know it will work.

How I overcame the credit mountain: A tale of credit success

Let me share one success story with you as proof of how your new knowledge and confidence can elevate your abilities to influence change. Last year I received a notice from a creditor that my account was 30 days past due. I was taken aback because I had never fallen 30 days behind. The notice indicated that my account had gone to the creditor's collection department.

Before I contacted the collection manager, I wanted to make sure my documentation was in place; therefore, I went to my bank's Website to verify the date that my November payment posted to my checking account.

I then called the collection manager to have the matter resolved. First, you must understand that in this type of situation you are automatically considered guilty in the eyes of your creditors and will be forced to prove your innocence.

Before divulging to the operator that I had already obtained proof that my payment was not late, I simply informed her that a mistake had obviously been made in their records. She curtly informed me that no mistake had occurred; rather, she said I just did not make the payment.

After going back and forth she placed me on hold and discovered that one of the payment processors had applied my payment to another accountholder's loan.

Astoundingly, she had the audacity to ask me to send her copies of paperwork I received from my bank. Obviously I didn't feel like it was my responsibility to help her remedy a mistake they had made, but I wanted the error corrected.

Her reply was: "In order to do that, it could take several days because I would have to retrieve the paperwork from archives." I reminded her of the credit union's obligation to correct it immediately and asked her to send me a letter on the company's letterhead explaining this error. I expected this to be corrected, but could not help being concerned that this issue would come back to haunt me; therefore, I made notes, documenting the date and nature of the conversation.

A few weeks passed and I had not received a response from the creditor. Concurrently, I had applied for credit and received a declination letter advising that my application could not be approved due to the presence of a recent delinquency appearing in my Trans Union credit report.

After receiving my credit report, I was not surprised to see a 30-day delinquency attached to one of my accounts. Yes, you guessed it, the same creditor that misapplied my November payment furnished the delinquency to Trans Union.

Concerned, I called the credit union but the employee had no prior record of me calling or of the processing error, and scolded me about missing a payment. The employee was the most rude and obnoxious individual that I have ever encountered in dealing with a creditor. I can remember her piercing words clearly: "It's not my fault you don't pay your bills on time."

As this was a local business, I gathered my documents, got dressed and drove to the creditor who had caused me so much distress. After meeting an account representative, I handed her all of my paperwork and she excused herself.

When she returned, she acknowledged that my payment had been misapplied. First, I requested a letter of correction on their letterhead and then I asked to speak with a manager. After I obtained my letter, I was introduced to the branch manager.

She apologized for the error but did not appear to be the least bit sincere. Walking in with a smirk on her face, I thought it was flippant that she did not seem to take their mistake seriously nor consider the negative impact it had on my credit.

I had to remind her of the inconvenience I had suffered (embarrassment, time off from work, denial of credit, and so on) as well as the violations to the Fair Credit Reporting Act that they had committed, including willful noncompliance and negligence.

As I left the credit union, I was doubtful that my experience would be shared with someone who could bring about a change in its processes (customer service and payment processing). So, I wrote a letter detailing everything that had occurred leading up to that day. I conveyed clearly how the credit union's negligence and failure to remedy the error had caused me hardship.

My letter also identified the specific laws that had been violated and expressed my intention to pursue litigation if they did not provide me with a letter of apology, correct my credit report immediately and provide evidence that their procedures would be reviewed and or changed.

Within three business days I had received two official letters from the president of the company. The first stated specifically that he had personally addressed the inadequate behavior displayed by his staff and, in particular, that of the collection manager. In addition, he apologized for the lack of professionalism she had displayed and advised that a review of their payment processing procedures was underway. I was also provided with an original correction letter (containing his signature) that was drafted and sent to all three of the national credit-reporting agencies. Lastly, he provided me with his direct telephone number and instructed me to contact him in the future in case I needed anything else.

As I read the letters, I was a bit disappointed that it took my own action to resolve the problem, but I also realized the importance of credit education. In the end, fairness had prevailed.

The bottom line to this story is that I knew what to do in the face of adversity because of my experience and credit knowledge. The president of the credit union (or someone who assisted him) realized that I was informed and that his business was at fault in a number of ways.

In the end, they acted swiftly to prevent the company from incurring any losses or bad publicity due to its negligence. The creditor exercised right action because it knew compelling evidence was obviously stacked against the company. Most importantly, someone knew that failure to honor my request could be detrimental and possibly yield severe consequences.

I assure you that you now have the power to raise standards in the same manner. This is only one success story. I have utilized my knowledge in helping friends and family take charge of their credit with credit-reporting agencies, collectors and creditors. Do not expect credit-reporting agencies or creditors to volunteer what your rights are or divulge what their responsibilities are with respect to credit reporting. You must know these things for yourself.

Avoid quoting credit laws when contacting credit-reporting agencies or lenders. Make your request and let the process run its course. Allow them the opportunity to either resolve the issue or fall short. If they fall short, then quote laws that they thought you were oblivious to.

This is also when you should contact the Federal Trade Commission and file a formal complaint and contact your attorney to seek litigation if necessary. Treat creditors in the same manner they treat you when you have not lived up to your end of an agreement with them. Remember, it's business—it's not personal.

Recovery is possible

If you are one of several consumers who have experienced credit problems, know that recovery is possible. You should begin with the understanding that a less than perfect credit rating is not the end of the world, nor is it the end of your chances to obtain credit. Like anything, your good credit status will return in time; however, time alone will not remedy the poor rating or prevent you from falling short again in the future.

It has been my experience that many consumers, even after improving a poor credit rating, will within a short time fall right back into the same pattern of behavior that brought about their poor credit to begin with. Poor credit is not always triggered by uncontrollable circumstances. More often than not it is related to a pattern of unhealthy financial/credit behavior that has been practiced for years.

The most important thing you can do to avoid regression is to focus on changing or eliminating bad habits. Stop being so dependent on credit! Develop strong relationships with your creditors in the beginning by making every attempt to pay on time. You must be consistent and pay on time. Doing so helps establish your good reputation and build trust with your creditors. This is the type of trust that influences creditors to waive a $35 late fee because one or two payments were paid after the due date.

This rapport is also what encourages creditors to restore your competitive rates instead of hiking them up to some astronomical percentage due to a missed or late payment. I tell you this from my own experience; I've lived it. Do not expect creditors to make provisions for you if you have consistently proved that you are not responsible by repeatedly defaulting on your debts.

Do not allow credit problems or slow payments to fester. Be proactive and let your debtors know as soon as possible when and how you plan on making payments, and then follow through. It is critical that you fulfill your end of the agreement. Do not ignore the creditors' calls or your due payments for months (or even years) and expect it to be easy to restore a good credit rating. Learn from the mistakes that contributed to you receiving poor ratings. Recognize them and do not repeat them!

For example, open your bills when you receive them. I am surprised at the number of consumers that allow their statements to sit on a desk or counter unopened for days upon days, sometimes even weeks. Failure to review them only exacerbates the current situation and prolongs the inevitable. Stop robbing Peter to pay Paul. This strategy will only ensure that someone will not get paid.

Don't forget to bargain

In closing, understand that everything is negotiable as long as each party has something to offer or can provide something that the other party needs. Use your knowledge and creativity to negotiate with lenders. When negotiating, make suggestions to your creditors. Counter an offer and learn how to say no. Do not expect creditors to reward you for paying your bills in full or on time. That is not realistic.

The possible outcomes of your negotiating include a "could have been better" result (when an agreement has been reached, but some elements of the desired outcome had to be sacrificed in order to reach the agreement), a win/lose result (when one party advances at the expense of the other), a lose/lose situation (when neither party obtains the desired outcome), or a win/win situation (when both parties have reached a desired outcome).

Let me demonstrate an example of each of these possible outcomes:

1. **Could have been better.** You negotiate to have a negative entry expunged from your credit record in return for payment to a creditor. The creditor would much rather receive payment and update your debt to reflect paid on your credit record. Removing accurate information in exchange for payment compromises the entire credit-reporting process and questions the integrity of consumer credit reports. It also solidifies a pattern of bad behavior and sets a dangerous precedent. Future lenders would be making decisions, in part, based on credit reports that are not accurate. Consumers will be less concerned with paying or paying on time because they can negotiate "clean" credit.

2. **Win/lose.** You repay a creditor and the creditor never updates your account to reflect a zero balance. The creditor's only motivation was receiving payment, not correcting your credit report. This furthers your disgust and distrust of the credit-reporting process and of creditors in general. As a result you are forced to contact the credit-reporting agencies on your own to correct your credit report.

3. **Lose/lose.** A creditor demands that you pay an amount that exceeds what you can afford or requires payment in a time frame that is unreasonable. Further, the creditor refuses to negotiate or accept a reasonable counteroffer. In this case, neither party obtains anything and the issue remains open. When this happens, go back to the drawing board and try to make your negotiations with another person in the creditor's organization.

4. **Win/win.** You establish an account with a creditor and fulfill the terms of the contract you signed by making all payments on time.

The creditor receives its money and you receive a positive repayment history on your credit report. This should always be the desired outcome both parties strive for.

No more excuses

Now that you have been exposed to an in-depth credit education, the burden of responsibility rests on you. No longer may you say, "I didn't know they could do that," "It's not fair" or "I don't understand how that works." What may have been an enigma to you previously should now be clear. You need only review and apply the knowledge that has been bestowed to you and you will be able to reap the rewards. If there is something that escaped you upon first reading, go back and study it again for comprehension.

Perhaps, more importantly, you now also have a responsibility to help educate and uplift your fellow consumers. Share the knowledge and experience you have gained from this material. Failure to do so would put you in the same category as some creditors and credit-reporting agencies who harbor pertinent information and make concerted efforts to conceal helpful data from the public. Take advantage of every opportunity you have to aid someone who is less-seasoned and more vulnerable than you. Pass on the truth. And what you cannot answer, research so that you will increase your knowledge and be able to respond in the future.

I hope that you've obtained a greater awareness from what you've read, and I hope this inspires you to be proactive in controlling your financial destiny. Although personal credit is only one portion of that journey, it is a significant leg. I hope this material has been informative and helpful in your quest to establish and maintain great credit and obtain financial freedom.

Appendix

Because contacting lenders, credit-reporting agencies, collectors and governmental offices can sometimes prove intimidating to consumers, I have prepared a number of examples you can follow to make the contact process easier. The following pages contain sample letters you can fit to your appropriate situation.

Disclosure request—denied credit

Date

Credit-Reporting Agency Name
Address Line 1
Address Line 2

Greeting:

I have recently been denied credit due in part to a report supplied by [credit agency Nname]. Please send me a free copy of my credit report as legislated by federal law. My personal information is as follows:

Your Full Name
Current Address Line 1
Current Address Line 2
Social Security Number
Date of Birth

Enclosed is a copy of the denial letter I received from [creditor's name], proof of my identity and proof of my current address.

Salutation,

Your Name

Disclosure request—fraud

Date

Credit-Reporting Agency Name
Address Line 1
Address Line 2

Greeting:

[Creditor or business name] has recently informed me that my personal information may have been compromised or used without my permission. Please send me a free copy of my credit report as legislated by federal law. My personal information is as follows:

Full Name
Current Address Line 1
Current Address Line 2
Social Security Number
Date of Birth

Enclosed is a copy of the letter I received from [creditor or business name], proof of my identity and proof of my current address.

Salutation,

Your Name

Disclosure request—unemployed

Date

Credit-Reporting Agency Name
Address Line 1
Address Line 2

Greeting:

I am currently unemployed and seeking employment. Please send me a free copy of my credit report as legislated by federal law. My personal information is as follows:

Full Name
Current Address Line 1
Current Address Line 2
Social Security Number
Date of Birth

Enclosed is proof of my identity and current address.

Salutation,

Your Name

Disclosure request—free state

Date

Credit-Reporting Agency Name
Address Line 1
Address Line 2

Greeting:

I currently reside in the state of [name of state]. Please send me a free copy of my credit report as legislated by state law. My personal information is as follows:

Full Name
Current Address Line 1
Current Address Line 2
Social Security Number
Date of Birth

Enclosed is proof of my identity and current address.

Salutation,

Your Name

Credit-reporting agency investigation request

Date

Credit-Reporting Agency Name
Address Line 1
Address Line 2

Greeting:

There are incorrect items listed on my credit report that I would like [credit-reporting agency's name] to research. My personal information is as follows:

Full Name
Current Address Line 1
Current Address Line 2
Social Security Number
Date of Birth

Enclosed is a list of the items that are inaccurate, proof of my identity and current address. Please send me a revised copy upon completion of your investigation.

Salutation,

Your Name

(List of inaccurate items)

Account Name	Account/Case Number	Dispute
Regal Bank	1012843995	Not my account.
Tri-City Auto	7281565002	Account never late.
Judgment for AAA	03105567	Case dismissed.
Cash Collectors	668943	Paid in full.

Disclosure request—fee enclosed

Date

Credit-Reporting Agency Name
Address Line 1
Address Line 2

Greeting:

Please send me a copy of my credit report as legislated by federal law. My personal information is as follows:

Full Name
Current Address Line 1
Current Address Line 2
Social Security Number
Date of Birth

Enclosed is a [check or money order] in the amount of [applicable charge], proof of my identity and current address.

Salutation,

Your Name

Opt-out request

Date

Credit-Reporting Agency Name
Address Line 1
Address Line 2

Greeting:

Please remove my name, address and telephone number from all marketing lists compiled by [credit reporting agency's name]. My personal information is as follows:

Full Name
Current Address Line 1
Current Address Line 2
Social Security Number
Date of Birth

Enclosed is proof of my identity and current address.

Salutation,

Your Name

Letter to creditor—reporting error

Date

Creditor's Name
Address Line 1
Address Line 2

Greeting:

[Creditor's name] has incorrectly reported to [credit-reporting agency's name] that my account [description of error]. Please correct this mistake with [credit-reporting agency's name] immediately and provide me with a document on [creditor's name] letterhead confirming the correction. My personal information is as follows:

Account Number
Full Name
Current Address Line 1
Current Address Line 2

Enclosed is proof of my identity and current address.

Salutation,

Your Name

Fraud or active duty alert request

Date

Credit-Reporting Agency Name
Address Line 1
Address Line 2

Greeting:

Please add a [fraud or active duty] alert to my credit report to assist in the prevention of unauthorized accounts being established in my identity.

My personal information is as follows:

Full Name
Social Security Number
Current Address Line 1
Current Address Line 2
Date of Birth

Enclosed is proof of my identity and current address. Please send me written confirmation that this request has been honored.

Salutation,

Your Name

Collection cease communication letter

Date

Collection Agency Name
Address Line 1
Address Line 2

Greeting:

Please discontinue all further contact with me regarding the debt listed below. Should [collection agency name] choose to ignore this request, I will take all necessary steps to protect my rights under applicable collection laws.

My personal information is as follows:

Full Name
Account Number
Current Address Line 1
Current Address Line 2

Salutation,

Your Name

Request to creditor for a reason of denial

Date

Creditor's Name
Address Line 1
Address Line 2

Greeting:

[Creditor's name] has recently declined my application for credit.
As legislated by federal law, please provide me with specific reasons
leading to this decision. My personal information is as follows:

Full Name
Current Address Line 1
Current Address Line 2
Date of Birth

Enclosed is a copy of the denial letter, as well as proof of my
identity and current address.

Salutation,

Your Name

Disclosure request—annual/complimentary

Date

Credit-Reporting Agency Name
Address Line 1
Address Line 2

Greeting:

Please send me a free, annual copy of my credit report as legislated by federal law. My personal information is as follows:

Full Name
Current Address Line 1
Current Address Line 2
Social Security Number
Date of Birth

Enclosed is proof of my identity and current address.

Salutation,

Your Name

Glossary

Account narrative: A remark or comment attached to a credit entry that provides additional details about the entry or its status. The comment may or may not impact a credit score and may be added by a furnisher or credit-reporting agency.

Annual percentage rate: The annual cost of a debt that normally includes interest and other fees such as transaction finance charges or origination fees.

Asset: Any item of real value that may be converted into cash.

Authorized: Designation assigned to a party who enters into a credit contract (usually credit card) under the condition that he or she may utilize the card to make purchases, but is not responsible for repayment of the monies.

Bankruptcy: Legal declaration stating that one is incapable of repaying monies owed to creditors.

Chapter 13: Type of bankruptcy that allows for the repayment of debts or liabilities through a wage earner plan.

Chapter 7: Type of bankruptcy in which one may be required to convert his or her assets into cash in order to repay or settle debts with creditors.

Check verification companies: Companies who are in the business of collecting check-writing patterns of consumers and making suggestions to merchants to accept or decline checks presented upon the data and risk associated.

Collection agency: An organization or attorney who is in the business of debt recovery. Usually such entities represent a client who they are collecting on behalf of.

Comaker: Same as cosigner.

Compliance: Adherence to credit laws (Fair Credit Reporting Act, Fair Debt Collection Practices Act, and so on) by credit-reporting agencies, creditors and other parties engaged in consumer credit reporting.

Consumer: Any individual for whom a credit record is maintained; a purchaser of any good or service.

Consumer credit counseling: A nonprofit organization that serves consumers in restructuring of finances and debt in order to repay creditors. They also provide finance education to consumers.

Consumer Data Information Association: A trade association that represents those businesses involved in the exchange of consumer information and regulated by the Fair Credit Reporting Act.

Consumer statement: Normally a 100-word statement written by consumers to provide further explanation about an entry or entries appearing on their credit reports. This statement may be edited for clarity by a credit-reporting agency and is available to creditors who access a consumer's credit file.

Cosigner: Designation assigned to a person who enters into a credit contract with another in which the cosigner agrees to repay the debt if the primary party defaults.

Credit: Something of value entrusted to another with the understanding of "receive now, pay later."

Credit doctor: A business that specializes in the practice of credit repair.

Credit file: Another name for a consumer credit report or credit record.

Credit repair: The act of either manipulating or finding loopholes in credit-reporting procedures in an effort to have legitimate credit entries and obligations removed from credit records.

Credit report: A summary of a consumer's repayment pattern and history maintained in a credit-reporting agency's database and made available to credit grantors in order to make credit decisions.

Credit-reporting agency: Unbiased repositories of consumer information.

Credit score: A numerical value used by lenders to help predict risk and future repayment performance.

Creditor: Any entity to whom money is due.

Discharged: The completion of a bankruptcy repayment plan (Chapter 13) or a final disposition assigned to a Chapter 7; it indicates settlement or exoneration of debts.

Dismissed: Refers to unsuccessful completion of a bankruptcy due to consumer withdrawal, or a final declaration by a court that a bankruptcy is not appropriate or adequate to remedy existing financial obligations. This determination remains on an individual's credit record for seven to 10 years.

Fair Credit Reporting Act: A federal body of law that regulates the credit-reporting industry and its participants with respect to fairness in practices to consumers.

Fair Debt Collection Practices Act: A body of law that regulates the practices and behaviors of collectors and helps ensure fair treatment to consumers.

Fair Isaac and Company: A company that designs scoring models and customizes them to meet the needs of various lenders and providers. Credit-reporting agencies offer them as tools to lenders for assessing the credit risks of consumers.

Federal Trade Commission: A governmental agency that enforces the Fair Credit Reporting Act.

Finance charge: Any charge (such as interest, late fees, and so on) levied for use of credit privileges.

Fraud alert: A message or flag attached to a consumer's credit record that asks creditors to seek additional information from an applicant before extending credit. It warns creditors that fraudulent, unauthorized applications may be submitted in a consumer's name.

Furnisher: Any entity who provides consumer-repayment information to a credit-reporting agency.

High credit: The highest amount that has been purchased or charged on a credit card account.

Identity theft: The illegal, unauthorized use of another's personal information in order to gain or benefit.

Identity theft insurance: A type of insurance available that covers many of the costs associated with or incurred while a consumer is trying to remedy damages resulting from identity theft.

Inquiry: A request for access to a consumer's credit report or a limited amount of information about a consumer that is made through a credit-reporting agency.

Installment credit: A type of credit in which the monthly repayment amount is constant (student loans and auto payments, for example).

Interest: The amount charged for the use of borrowed money. This amount is typically expressed as the annual percentage rate of a principal balance.

Interest rate: The interest per year divided by the principal amount of a debt, expressed as a percentage.

Joint: A designation assigned to parties who enters into a credit contract with equal repayment responsibilities.

Judgment: A legal decision or court order to pay or fulfill a financial obligation to another party.

Last activity date: Commonly called "date of last activity," this refers to the original delinquency date of an unrecovered account, the date of last payment or transaction or the date an account is closed.

Liabilities: The amount of financial obligation an individual is responsible for repaying.

Lien: A claim on a property as security for the payment of a just debt. Liens are filed in state and federal courts for payment due relative to income or property taxes.

Maker: The designation assigned to a person who enters into a credit contract as the signer of a promissory note.

North American Link: Shared system or database that allows North American merchants and creditors to receive information regarding a consumer's credit accounts originating in another North American country (for example, the United States and Canada).

Open credit: The type of credit in which the total balance incurred for a billing period must be repaid at the end of the billing cycle (for example, mobile phones, gas cards and utilities).

Preapproved: A prescreened offer of credit sent to consumers from merchants or creditors. This offer is based upon limited general information about a consumer's credit behavior and does not indicate a firm offer of credit.

Principal: The amount borrowed (or portion of that amount) that has not yet been repaid. The principal amount is exclusive of associated interest fees.

Public records: This refers to proceedings or events recorded in court that are open to the public (for example, divorces, bankruptcies, liens, judgments or garnishments).

Reason-code: An explanation generated by a credit scoring model and usually related to the contributing factor(s) for the declination of credit (or one that resulted in a lower score than possible).

Reinsertion: Refers to the process of a creditor or credit-reporting agency resubmitting a credit entry that was previously removed from a consumer's credit records.

Reinvestigation: The process of a credit-reporting agency verifying the accuracy of a credit entry (or another segment of information) appearing on a consumer credit report.

Released: Term assigned to a state or federal lien that has been paid.

Retention: The length of time an entry legally remains on a consumer credit file.

Revolving credit: The type of credit that requires a minimum monthly payment. In this case, the minimum could change based upon the total debt balance (charge card and department store cards).

Satisfied: The term assigned to a judgment that has been paid.

Secured credit: A form of credit that requires a contribution from a consumer. This contribution serves as security, ensuring repayment if the account holder fails to make payment.

Shared: The designation assigned to persons who enter into a credit contract with equal repayment responsibilities.

Terms: The amount of monthly payment or the number of months or years a loan is scheduled for repayment.

Undesignated: A designation assigned to an account in which the primary and secondary persons responsible for repayment are not identified.

References

Bankruptcy Law Firms. Available online at:
  www.bankruptcylawfirms.com. 2004.

Consumer Data Industry Association. Available online at:
  www.cdiaonline.com. 2003.

Cornell University. Available online at: *www.cornell.edu.* 2003.

Equifax. Available online at: *www.equifax.com.* 2004.

Experian. Available online at: *www.experian.com.* 2004.

Fair Credit Reporting Act. Available online at: *www.fcraclassaction.com.* 2003.

Federal Trade Commission. Available online at: *www.ftc.gov.* 2004.

Hagenbaugh, Barbara. "Consumer debt loads at record. What happens when interest rates rise?" *USA Today.* 9 May 2004.

Hwang, Suein. "Once-Ignored Consumer Debts Are Focus of Booming Industry." *Wall Street Journal.* 25 October 2004, (A11).

Insurance Information Institute. Available online at: *www.iii.org.* 2003.

Kozicki, Stephen. *Creative Negotiating.* Mass.: Adams Media Corporation, 1998.

Lahart, Justin. "Spending our way to disaster." *CNN Money.* (2003). 9 May 2004. *http://money.cnn.com/2003/10/02/markets/consumerbubble.*

Laurier, Joanne. "US consumer debt reaches record levels." *World Socialist Website* (2004). 9 May 2004. *http://wsws.org/articles/2004/jan2004/debt-j15_prn.shtml.*

National Foundation for Credit Counseling. Available online at: *www.nfcc.org.* 2003.

New World Dictionary of The American Language (1984, second college edition). New York: New World Dictionaries.

Sidel, Robin. "Banks, Customers Adapt to Paperless Check Processing." *Wall Street Journal.* 10 October 2004, B1 +.

Simons, David. "Id Theft Insurance Isn't Insurance." *Forbes.* May 2003. Accessed online, 12 June 2003.

http://www.forbes.com/2003/05/29/cx_ds_0529simons.html.

Simons, David. "Make Your Identity Useless To Thieves." *Forbes.* June 2003.

http://www.forbes.com/2003/06/12/cx_ds_0612simons.html.

Stanley, Thomas J. (2001). *The Millionaire Mind*. Andrews McMeel Publishing.

Stern, Linda. "Scoring A First Loan." *Newsweek.* 20 September 2004: 58.

The American Heritage Dictionary of the English Language (2000, fourth edition). Boston: Houghton Mifflin Company.

Trans Union. Available online at: *www.transunion.com.* 2004.

Index

A

accounts, types of
    checking, 115
    installment, 26, 60-61
    joint, 215-219
    open, 26, 60-61
    revolving, 28, 60-61, 112
    savings, 115
active duty alerts, 172-173
alerts, types of
    active duty, 172-173
    fraud, 43, 168, 172
Anderson Financial Network, 235
Asset Acceptance Management, 235
authorized users, 37

B

balances, transferring, 43
bankruptcy, 39, 95, 63-66, 215-216

Beacon, 102, 104
billing errors, 205-206
bounced checks, 233-234

C

car dealerships, 47, 122-124
car loans, late payments on, 127-128
car shopping, negotiating, 122-124
CCCS, 148
Certegy, 226
Chapter 11 bankruptcy, 63-66
Chapter 12 bankruptcy, 63-66
Chapter 13 bankruptcy, 63-66
Chapter 7 bankruptcy, 63-64
Check 21, 232-234
check verification companies,
    225-229
checking accounts, 115

checks, bounced, 233-234

child support, 197

civil liberties, 200-202

collection agencies, 206-211, 234-236
    bargaining with, 128-129

collection reports, 94

Consumer Credit Protection Act, 206-211

Consumer Data Industry Association, 224-225

consumer statements, 44-45

consumers, role in credit-reporting system, 25-26

co-signing for credit, 36-37, 45

counselors, credit, 24-25
    finding, 147-155
    guidelines for, 150-151

court orders, 194-195

credit,
    applying for, 39-45
    basic types of, 26-28
    co-signing for, 36-37, 45
    definition of, 19-22
    denial of, 54
    establishing, 35-38, 230-231
    joint, 36, 39
    preapproved offers for, 38
    reestablishing, 39-43, 45-47

credit card balances, transferring, 43

credit cards, applying for, 124

credit checks, avoiding, 47

credit clinics. *See* credit doctors

credit counselors, 24-25
    finding, 147-155
    guidelines for, 150-151

credit doctors, 179-187

credit fraud, utilities and, 76

Credit Repair Organization Act, 185, 187

credit reports, 57-59
    disputing, 133-142
    obtaining, 53-56, 174
    reinsertion of items on, 180, 186, 193-194
    reinvestigations and, 191-193
    retention of information on, 59-66
    viewing online, 134

credit score, 47, 99-109
    factors that affect, 104-107, 153-154
    importance of, 100-104
    improving your, 109-113
    obtaining, 174

credit-counseling services, 148

credit-reporting agencies, 22-23, 83-84
    contacting, 28-30, 56-57
    history of, 84-86
    importance of, 87-90, 92-95

credit-reporting system, major players in, 20, 22-26

D

debt,
  paying off, 42-43
  shared, 39
debt management, 24-25, 149, 153-154
deposits, security, 74
Direct Marketing Association, 199
direct marketing lists, 95, 198-200
  removing your contact information from, 174
direct-to-consumer products, 93
discharged vs. dismissed bankruptcies, 64-65
dispute letters, 136
disputes, unresolved, 141-142
divorce, 39, 197
Dun & Bradstreet, 23

E

electronic checks. *See* Check 21
employer ID numbers, 181-182
employers, credit checks and, 195
E-Oscar, 224
Equal Credit Opportunity Act, 203-204
Equifax, 23, 29, 53, 92-93, 95, 168, 226-229
exchanges, on goods, 74-75
Experian, 23, 29, 53, 113-115, 168
Experian/Fair Isaac Risk Model, 102, 104

F

Fair and Accurate Credit Transactions Act, 54, 55, 172-176
Fair Credit Billing Act, 204-206
Fair Credit Reporting Act, 24, 29, 61, 78-79, 134, 139, 142, 172-175, 180-181, 191-198, 200-202, 209, 225
Fair Debt Collection Practices Act, 128, 206-211
Fair Isaac and Company, 101, 115
Federal Bureau of Investigation (FBI), 200-202
Federal Trade Commission, 24, 25-26, 61, 79, 139-141, 162, 164, 174, 184-185, 192, 204, 209-211, 224
finance charges, calculating, 41
firm credit inquiries, 22
firm offer of credit, 197-198
floating, 233-234
foreign countries, establishing credit in, 230-231
fraud, 90-92, 95
  defining, 162-167
  police reports and, 169-179
  reporting, 167-170
fraud alerts, 43, 168, 172
furnishers, 23-24

G

garnishments, 63
goods, exchanging, 74-75

H

home loans, late payments and,
    127-128

I

ICR Services. *See* Nationwide
    Credit Repair
ID numbers, 181-182
Identity Theft Affidavit, 168-169
identity theft,
    credit reports and, 174
    credit scores and, 174
    defining, 162-167
    insurance for, 170-171
    police reports and, 169-179, 225
    reporting, 167-170
    statistics for, 165-167
    utilities and, 76
Identity Theft Clearinghouse,
    164-165
Innovis Consumer Assistance,
    231-232
inquiries, soft vs. firm, 22
installment accounts, 26, 60-61
insurance, identity theft, 170-171
interest rates, negotiating and,
    125-126
interest, calculating, 41

J

joint credit, 36, 39, 215-219
judgments, 63

L

late payments, 126-128
liens, 62-63
loans,
    co-signing for, 36-37, 45
    paying off, 42-43
    types of, 127-128

M

Millionaire Mind, The, 30
Millionaire Next Door, The, 30

N

National Credit Education and
    Review. *See* Nationwide
    Credit Repair
National Foundation for Credit
    Counseling, 148-152
Nationwide Credit Repair, 184-185
NCO Group, Inc., 210-211
negotiating skills, 121-129, 249-251
NFCC, 148-152
North American Link, 230-231

O

online shopping, 91
open accounts, 26, 60-61

P

Patriot Act, 200-202
payments, making late, 126-128
Permissible Purposes, 194-197, 200
personal loans, late payments and, 127-128
police reports, identity theft and, 169-179, 225
Portfolio Recovery, 235
portfolio-management tools, 95
preapproved credit offers, 38
promotional marketing lists, 174, 198-200

R

reason-codes, 107
reinsertion, 180, 186, 193-194
reinvestigation, 133-142, 191-193
    requesting via computer, 138
    requesting via mail, 135-136
    requesting via telephone,137-138
    unresolved, 141-142
retention rules, 71
re-verification requests, 60
revolving accounts, 28, 60-61, 112

S

Scorex PLUS, 113-114
scoring models, 101-109
section 604. *See* Permissible Purposes
security deposits, 74
September 11th, 200-202, 232
shared credit. *See* joint credit
Social Security Administration, 160, 181
Social Security numbers, 159-162, 173
soft credit inquiries, 22
Stanley, Thomas J., 30
statements, consumer, 44-45

T

tax ID numbers, 181-182
telecommunication service providers, 78-79
telemarketing, 95, 174, 198-200
telephone services, 78-79
terrorism, 200-202
Trans Union, 23, 30, 53, 168
Truth in Lending Act, 204-206

U

U.S. government, role in credit-reporting system, 24
Uniform Code of Military Justice, 201

universal default clause, 196

utilities, and credit fraud/
   identity theft, 76

utility service providers, 78-89

utility services, establishing, 73-79

About the Author

K.E. Varner is a former instructor and vendor manager for Equifax, one of the major information services companies and national credit-reporting agency. During his tenure, he trained and developed customer service personnel, functioned as subject matter expert on a number of business projects, represented the company in federal court during consumer/credit-reporting agency mediation and facilitated credit industry information to organizations such as the Atlanta Housing Authority.

He is a member of the following consumer interest groups: National Association of Consumer Agency Administrators, National Association of Consumer Advocates and the American Council on Consumer Interests.

K.E. Varner currently works and resides in Norcross, Georgia, where he's a leader in Nextel's Customer Experience Quality group.